An Elegant Mind's Handbook

By
Paula D. Tozer

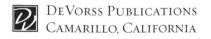

DeVorss Publications
Camarillo, California

An Elegant Mind's Handbook
Copyright © 2020 by Paula D. Tozer

Library of Congress Catalog Number: 2020934113
First Printing, 2020

PRINT ISBN: 978-087516-909-5
EBOOK ISBN: 978-087516-910-1

DeVorss & Company, Publisher
PO Box 1389
Camarillo CA 93012
www.devorss.com

Table of Contents

Preface

I believe that every person alive has elegance within. The creative impulse to explore, discover our personal potential, and expand our awareness is our birthright as human beings. We are worthy of this wonder, this exquisite elegance, simply by being born.

However, the vast majority of us have had our creative potential devalued to the point where we feel it is non-existent. We have been trained to believe the voice of fear and ignore the voice of our true nature.

So much loss, death, and turmoil in my life led me to a place where I felt I had nothing left to lose, so I decided to try something new.

With *An Elegant Mind's Handbook*, I ventured into my inner wilderness to discover my essential nature. I ignored the voice of fear and let my creativity take over. I began to practice what I now call contemplative writing. Nothing was taboo. The voice of my true nature provided a trail of words that led me to the Wellspring of Inspiration, a space of infinite possibility.

The voice of my true nature has become my Constant Traveler.

Fifteen years ago, I set out to become friends with my Constant Traveler.

She was always with me. If I hiked to the top of a mountain, she was there. Sunbathing on a beach in the Dominican Republic, she was there with me. As I worked and played and mothered, wife'd and sister'd and daughter'd, she was there. She was my constant companion.

Yep, she was me.

Fifteen years ago, I realized that I didn't know myself very well at all, because I didn't have a clue how to be her friend. However, I did know one thing—how to abuse her. My inner voice was harsh. It bullied me. It guilt-tripped-me-up at every opportunity. It made me the Queen of Shoulda, Woulda, Coulda Land. My inner voice forced me to take everything personally.

There was one saving grace in my inner life—the creativity that allowed me to dream. It kept the door to possibilities open just a crack, enough for me to receive what I began to understand as "flashes of brilliance."

One day, in a flash of brilliance, I realized that the harsh inner voice wasn't my own. It sounded very much like what other people had said to me over the years. I was a bit freaked out by this revelation! Fascinated, I chose to examine this realization on a deeper level.

So I sat silently and listened, but not with my ears.... I listened with my heart. Compassion for the woman who is me began to fill me. My heart invited me to be curious, playful, excited, and passionate. An inner voice that sounded very much like my own invited me to write.

An interesting thing happened when I took up that invitation. The harsh voice that I thought was my own began to sound gentler and kinder. Her language changed too as I began to look at my beliefs, values, and assumptions with a gentle, open heart. It transformed into what I could only describe as elegant.

She is now my friend. I know her as my Constant Traveler— the most compassionate, honorable, and elegant expression of me that I can imagine. I know now that through it all, she has always had my back. I had to stop talking and learn how to listen to her.

The commentary included in the statements of *An Elegant Mind's Handbook* are conversations with my Constant Traveler. They are as close to true as I can possibly come at this point in my life. I offer them to you for your consideration. You may agree. You may disagree.

That is not the point, as I see it. The point is to create a mindspark, a moment of insight, that allows you to connect with your own Constant Traveler, and to examine what you believe and value from the perspective of your own elegant mind.

> *Out beyond ideas of wrongdoing and rightdoing*
> *there is a field. I'll meet you there.*
> —Rumi

That is where you and I connect. Elegance, our true nature, is the field where all minds become One.

—Paula D. Tozer

An Elegant Mind's Handbook

Elegance Is...

Elegance is the natural expression of inner wealth. It is innate, universal, and observable. It is who you are before you have a chance to think about it and decide otherwise. Elegance is not learned. All things are made of it; it is a building block of being.

The expression of elegance is not limited to human beings but includes all beings and all things. Each possesses that which it is—vibrant energy, natural flow, and authenticity. Elegance is demonstrated in a bird's song, in the lithe, fluid movement of a mountain lion, within a gnarled, ancient apple tree standing stark against the sky. It is delivered by a mare's tail cloud, by deep ocean waves crashing on a rocky shore, on the back of a neon green beetle that finds its way inside my house.

The interesting thing about elegance is that human beings are the only beings who forget to remember what is so blatantly obvious to all other aspects of nature. Nature knows, because elegance is pure living. Why is this? Perhaps because they don't spend precious time considering an alternative, expending an extraordinary amount of energy attempting to persuade others of what they are not.

SACRED SIMPLICITY...

Among other descriptors, the dictionary describes *elegance* as simplicity. It shows up as clean lines, clarity, and genuineness. It is not acquired or learned. It is intrinsic.

Our world is full of complexities, convolutions, and confusions. They catch us up in a cyclone of thoughts and emotions, and we never seem to touch down, to feel solid ground under our feet. It is scary stuff.

WOULDN'T IT BE NICE TO HAVE THAT CYCLONE CEASE?

Consider those things you hold sacred in your life. I think that once you begin to look for them, you will find that they are quite basic. Holding the goal of simplicity in our minds can slow the whirlwind.

Elegance is the natural expression of a beautiful mind; it is the result of focused intention. It is demonstrated when we resist the temptation to "wallow in the mire" of negative, destructive thoughts and instead lift our being with mastery and majesty to where we can see the panoramic view.

CONTEMPLATION...

We live our lives at the whim of our emotions and think this is all there is to life. We perceive and react as we get pulled in by the undertow of life's drama. To understand the chaos of strong emotion—to calm the waters and allow us to see clearly to the bottom of the pool—there is contemplation.

Contemplation is a form of meditation, of becoming familiar with our mind. By considering an idea or thought and chewing on it in order to savor its flavor, we are allowing the monkey chatter that can overwhelm our consciousness to subside.

An Elegant Mind's Handbook is the result of over fifteen years of study, questioning, and contemplation. It represents my focused efforts to summarize that which I had come to hold as sacred into concise statements of elegant simplicity.

This text is by no means complete, no more complete than my life is complete. In this volume I expand upon each statement as it comes through my dialogues with my Constant Traveler. I offer them to you as a beginning for your personal dialogue with your own Constant Traveler.

Contemplation is a space in which you may be intimately familiar or where you may not have visited until now. Either way, it has been waiting for you.

Living in the Gap

Between stimulus and response there is a space. In that space is our power to choose our response. In our response lies our growth and our freedom. —Viktor E. Frankl

As Frankl notes, there is a gap between something that provokes a response in you and your response. OK, it may be only a second or two, but it is there. That gap is your power. You can make the choice to stretch out that gap, to make it longer. In the gap you have choices. Become mindful of this gap and give it your full attention.

When faced with a challenging situation, an elegant mind uses discretion and discernment. It takes the time required to respond in a mature manner. Psychologists call this self-regulation. Responding instead of reacting is what it means to live in the gap. Reaction is acting instinctively, based on emotion. Response is acting executively, based on wisdom. The gap is where we determine if we are a follower or a leader—a queen, a king, or a pawn.

If you travel to London and take the underground subway system, you will be reminded often to "Mind the Gap."

First introduced in 1968, this now famous phrase cautions travelers, audibly or visually, to pay attention when crossing the gap between the train door and the station platform.

Consider how signs and symbols for elegant living are everywhere if we train ourselves to look for them...

Be mindful: The gap is where we transform reaction into response.

An Elegant Mind...

1

An Elegant Mind Loves Wide Open.

Love's return is not its concern.

What is love? Can you know love by comparing it to what it is not? Love does not compare to anything. There are no degrees of true love—that is why it is called unconditional. There are, however, degrees of special love, attached love, and dependent love.

What does it mean to love wide open? Wide-open love is love without attachments. You are not attached to any gain or outcome when you love wide open—you just let whatever comes flow through. Wide open means you are simply expressing your nature as a human being. You hold nothing back. The return on this investment is the realization of your own potential.

To explore this and understand it as our foundation, what you are truly expressing as you live each day, you must go beyond the conventional way of thinking. Words are symbols for the feeling our thoughts incite. Our thoughts allude to something even deeper. In this manner, consider compassion (the desire to relieve suffering and give joy) as being synonymous with unconditional love.

Compassion begins with you. You cannot share that which is not yours to give. Authentic compassion for yourself will gradually mature into compassion for others as you realize that others are really the same as you—when you understand that everyone, at some point in their life, has suffered.

This means you must respect yourself, the quality of your thoughts, and your personal autonomy regarding loving. You must respect the autonomy of others more than you value your interpretation of love by offering it without expectation of return.

LOVE IS, REGARDLESS OF YOUR PERCEPTION OF IT...

Love is always simply love, regardless of the myriad forms in which it manifests. It is you who confuses love when you taint it with fear of its loss. It, however, remains constant. Its expansive nature extends itself by limitless sharing.

WOULD YOU BE OFFERING LOVE IF YOU PLACED ANY LIMITS ON IT?

The folks who live as close to true love as humanly possible do not feel the compulsion to say it is so. They are living examples of love, so in tune with their essence that its fragrance attracts everyone. They offer it free of charge and expect nothing in return. *Return is not a concern*, as they are too focused on what they are extending to be concerned about what is reflected. They are in love with the way the light plays off all that they see.

A Constant Traveler Reminder:
LOVE WIDE OPEN

What does loving wide open look like in your life? Flesh it out in point by point form. Dream bigger than you have before. Describe a scenario where you would be loving without attachment to an outcome.

Give someone you know some TLC.

Eventually, you will come to understand that love heals everything, and love is all there is.

—Gary Zukav

2

An Elegant Mind Knows That Freedom from Limitation Is Attainable...

...and that its pursuit is worthwhile.

The universe is an infinite source of wealth and knowledge, available to anyone. With an elegant mind, you are able to tap into this vision of freedom at any time, knowing that no matter what problem or limitation you are experiencing, there is a solution waiting to connect with you.

THE ELEGANT MIND'S CHOICE...

You have been creating the vision for your life all your life. Your past choices and your experiences based on those choices have brought you here. What does your best life look like? To be free to pursue your best life, you must hold the vision of it in your mind: what it looks like, what it feels like, what it sounds like as you describe it. Be prepared to accept the changes your vision will require of you.

CHANGE OR RESISTANCE?

Life is change. It is the only constant in life. Regardless of our protestations, it is impossible to not be subject to the changes that come with time. Resistance to change manifests as stagnation and regression. These can bring on stress and disease.

EMBRACING CHANGE...

Elegance is acceptance of the natural flow of thoughts and events. With time comes the opportunity to discover and understand the elegance of your own mind with greater clarity. The possibilities are endless.

Your choice to mount an expedition of self-discovery is the genesis of possibility. All new discoveries begin with the inspiration of the explorer—you must first imagine it possible.

You place limitations on yourself when you judge each thought, each word, each action as worthy or unworthy. Begin by practicing observation of your thoughts without any intention, evaluation, or reaction. This can be achieved through contemplation and meditation.

To live your best life, it is necessary to value each achievement. A beginning effort slowly and surely builds momentum.

KNOW THAT WHAT YOU KNOW IS NOT ALL THERE IS TO KNOW...

You accumulate information every day in the form of experience. Looking back at your life, you can acknowledge that you know more than you did when you were a kid, even if you simply call that knowledge *experience*, even if all you know for sure is, "I won't do that again."

How do you know what you know? Do you believe you are wiser than you were last year? Ten years ago?

You have been thinking within the confines of rules, boundaries, and limitations all your life. Many of these were adaptations designed to keep you safe, but many no longer serve you. Perhaps it is time to offer yourself the freedom to choose otherwise?

THE CHOICE TO WALK CREATES THE PATH AHEAD...

Consider your choices as a series of luminous stepping-stones that are powered not by the sun but by your intention. They extend in all directions but light up only when they sense your attention and energy. When you make the move, the step responds and lights up.

Consider the smallest obstacle you have overcome, and begin there. Freedom can be accomplished one gentle step at a time. Each step is the springboard for the next one—it energizes and forms the next step.

Understanding freedom from limitation does not have to be overwhelming; it can be done in increments. Envision a gently sloping pathway of easily navigated steps—a stairway designed to build confidence and staying power.

Have you ever...?
- Lost a pound
- Taken a course and passed it
- Made a new recipe
- Sung a song (and not just in the shower)
- Spoken up for yourself
- Assembled an IKEA product
- Learned to play guitar

ITS PURSUIT IS WORTHWHILE...

Pursuit, in this regard, is an activity (an occupation, career, interest, etc.) to which one devotes time and energy. Success can be achieved in the same manner as a baby learning to walk (baby steps), approaching it with the four Fs—*fearless, faith, focus,* and *fortitude:*

• **Fearless**—because when you practice doing something you fear, you begin to fear it less and less. This is the genesis of confidence.

• **Faith**—that the Wellspring of Inspiration is open to all, always and in all ways. It is through inspiration that you create the vision of your best life.

• **Focus**—the result of inspiration that sustains your intention and attention as you advance with confidence toward the vision of your best life.

• **Fortitude**—as, expressing the spirit of a Michelangelo, you keep your *eyes on the prize*, chipping away at the block of stone, gradually revealing the work of art underneath, the work of art that is your life.

It would be overwhelming to implement these suggestions all at once, but perhaps one per week is achievable?

A Constant Traveler Reminder:

ACTIVATE THE NEW 1% RULE

To change your life 100% *right now* would be overwhelming, but to implement change in 1% increments, weekly, is quite attainable. And after one year, you would have changed your life by 52%. These are the *minimum* results you can expect, because change can build in momentum, and quantum leaps are possible.

Need help deciding where to focus your efforts? Consider Stephen Covey's Time Management Matrix (Put First Things First) in his business classic *The 7 Habits of Highly Effective People*, where he states that our efforts can be organized into four quadrants:

1. **Urgent and Important** (items requiring our immediate attention)
2. **Important but Not Urgent** (items that are vital to achieving our long-term goals)
3. **Urgent but Not Important** (interruptions or distractions to be minimized or eliminated)
4. **Not Urgent and Not Important** (time wasters to be minimized or eliminated)

In this way you can determine the priority of each task and plan accordingly. Set a goal. Make a list of small things you can do toward that goal. Slot time on your calendar for them. Check them off when you have completed them. After you have completed five small tasks, reward yourself. Rock on!

3

An Elegant Mind Knows It May Forget to Remember Its Elegance from Time to Time.

UNCONDITIONAL POSITIVE REGARD...

C arl Rogers was a brilliant man and an accomplished psychologist. He was nominated for a Nobel Peace Prize in 1987 for his work in conflict resolution in South Africa and Ireland. His concept of *unconditional positive regard* is a pillar of ethical psychology.

To Rogers, unconditional positive regard meant approaching each one-on-one encounter, each relationship, with the spirit of unconditional acceptance of that person as a human being. This did not mean he condoned their misbehavior or abuses (of themselves or others), but it did mean that he believed in the inherent goodness of that person. He stood firm in the knowing that they had an elegant spirit within, an elegance of which they may not be aware.

Unconditional positive regard was the translation of his belief in the possibilities inherent in that person. Rogers masterfully led his clients to discover their personal elegance.

Unconditional PERSONAL regard...

My thoughts on this have extended to embrace what I term as becoming friends with my Constant Traveler. That person is the one who, no matter how far I go, how fast I get there, or how busy I am, remains forever in a one-on-one, face-to-face encounter with—*myself*. I have found this relationship works best when I offer myself unconditional personal regard.

This means giving myself a break when I react in a way that is unbecoming of an elegant being—when I forget to remember, in the heat of the moment, who I am.

In those moments when I don't have to be *that way* or say *that thing* but I feel like doing so, and I can, I do. When I criticize or condemn myself or someone else. When I tend to raise my voice—or even my hand—in anger, surprise, envy, or fear. When I am feeling cranky, scratchy, or hateful, and I don't *feel* like giving someone the best of me, I don't.

But most especially in those times, when I come face-to-face with the fact that it's easier to say "You don't know me" and blame someone else for my lack of elegance, it is time to remember that *I'm the one* who forgot who *I am*.

Especially then.

Everything gently...

Most times the person we are hardest on is ourself. We berate ourselves for things for which we easily let others off the hook. We all take wrong turns. We stumble and fall. There is nobody alive who has not taken a wrong turn at one time or another. When you mess up, you step up. You own it, but it does not serve you to hang on to it. Steppin' up can be simple but not easy. The elegant mind gently learns from its missteps and keeps on steppin'.

ONE ACT OF ELEGANCE CAN CHANGE YOUR WORLD.
IT IS ALWAYS THE ELEGANT CHOICE TO PRACTICE
DOING EVERYTHING GENTLY...

A Constant Traveler Reminder:
EVERYTHING GENTLY

Post this "Everything Gently Reminder" wherever you need to see it. The printable file may be downloaded at pauladtozerauthor.com.

Everything Gently Reminder

Feeling anxious? Overwhelmed? Impatient?

STOP. ▷ Take a short break.

LOOK ▷ Observe your situation. Give yourself some space.

LISTEN ▷ Listen to your inner dialogue. Take a few deep breaths and relax your muscles while repeating... "Everything Gently..."

Resume your day with the intention of doing every aspect of life gently

4

An Elegant Mind Recognizes Its Connection to the Wellspring of Inspiration.

It shares this connectivity like ripples
on water in order that all may partake.

There is a Wellspring of Inspiration so vast it is infinite.
It is discovered in the dark of night more often
than found in the light of day.
It defies definition by offering its possibilities
in endless, effervescent expression.
Mind-shifters live there.
We know these ones as artists.
We are all artists.

THE WELLSPRING OF INSPIRATION IS AVAILABLE TO
ALL AND THROUGH ALL, ALWAYS...

Creating a lovely song is art. Painting a beautiful picture is art. Writing a thoughtful poem is art. Telling a story that touches the heart is art. And living...living is an art.

23

ARTFUL LIVING CONNECTS ME TO MY PERSONAL
VERSION OF INSPIRATION...

Inspiration must be shared to be known, as it is realized only through sharing. A best life is demonstrated through Artful Living by mastering and integrating the gentle, elegant arts:
- Appreciation—the greatest, the foundation of the other arts
- Forgiveness
- Compassion
- Acceptance
- Freedom
- Patience
- Humility
- Silence
- Trust

WHERE IS THE JOY OF A SONG, THE DELIGHT IN A POEM,
A TALE, A HEART...A LIFE...IF IT IS NOT SHARED
SO THAT ALL MAY REJOICE?

A Constant Traveler Reminder:
ELEGANT ART

Select one of the elegant arts from the list above.
Practice it today. Each new day this week,
select another one.

5

An Elegant Mind Recognizes the Inherent Dignity of All Living Beings.

It always chooses the compassionate course of action.

As you breathe in, cherish yourself. As you breathe out, cherish all Beings. —His Holiness the Dalai Lama

A couple of years ago, I happened upon an online exchange among some individuals, part of a group who gathered on LinkedIn to discuss spiritual concepts. It was a no-holds-barred sparring match between the Vegetarians and Vegans vs. the Carnivores. It began and ended as a heated, passionate debate, each side offering their perspective with well-seated vigor. Neither side won. Each retreated to their respective corner to feast upon their personal righteousness.

When the Carnivores left the conversation, the dialogue continued between the Vegetarians and the Vegans. In what seemed to be a smug manner, they extolled the virtues of a plant-based diet. However, a few more posts into the exchange, one Vegetarian offered his current menu as ideal. He stated that even though he primarily consumed plants, beans, nuts, and seeds, to find easy sources of complete protein, he often included eggs, cheese, and occasionally fish in his diet.

This, as one of my old bosses used to say, changed the water on the beans.

The strict Vegans began to close ranks. Sentences became decidedly succinct. The noose grew tighter as another argument, albeit an organic one, began to sprout. To placate all concerned (or maybe to stir things up—it was hard to tell), an individual offered that even eating plants was killing.

Herbicide? Even from my remote ringside observation post, I could hear the collective intake of breath.

Subsequent posts came in short bursts. Each person offered the snippet of philosophy with which they justified their consumption of vegetables and herbs that were as garden fresh and close to live as humanly possible. The exchange became painful as each one struggled to justify their most primary need—that of survival. Truly it was a matter of life and death.

Reading this exchange made a distinct impression on me. I am not a voyeur in this debate.

I DO NOT LIVE TO EAT, BUT LIKE EVERY HUMAN ALIVE,
I DO EAT TO LIVE...

It got me thinking about our very human tendency to justify and confirm our outlook on life from our unique perspective. No one with a smidgen of compassion in their heart would ever condone the mistreatment of animals in any setting, even an industrial-farming operation. Nor would many have the constitution with which to slaughter the beasts whose flesh they regularly consume. For most it would be traumatic to even consider the happenings in a slaughterhouse, let alone slaughter the animals themselves. However, both situations exist as a direct result of our shared humanity. Mine and yours.

Each day we feed our pretty pet goldfish and then dig into our salmon dinner with sweet anticipation. We post pictures of Sadie, our pet potbellied pig, on Facebook, while we slow-cook pork ribs for the evening's meal—even as we turn up our nose in disgust when we think of people eating those animals we consider pets.

We cannot eat the living beings we name, so we distance ourselves from the barn to be able to consume that animal once it is slaughtered. We cultivate and nurture our tropical plants, while we drive over others with our tractors and tillers and poison still others to make our gardens fit our definition of beauty. Even those sincere pesticide-free advocates routinely kill thousands of living plants each year to sustain their lives.

These contradictions—the means leading up to the consumer's most enjoyable ends—are most often ignored. We value life when it serves us. It is a matter of degree.

ARE THERE DEGREES TO LIFE? WHICH EXPRESSION OF LIFE IS MORE VALUABLE?

Life is relationship. For us to live, something must die. From the air we breathe (we consume oxygen) to every morsel of sustenance we ingest (plant or flesh) to the very organism we inhabit, we consume fuel to fire our internal systems. We host bacteria that keep us healthy by scavenging upon other bacteria. The flora and fauna within our bodies enact a continuous cycle of eat-and-be-eaten with our every heartbeat. This distasteful reality of life as we know it is the essence of our conflict, both intrinsic and extrinsic. We are consumers.

We are, indeed, insatiable consumers.

Every time we go for a walk or get behind the wheel of our car, we kill whatever bug, worm, butterfly, or bird that has the misfortune of being in our path. Every time we sterilize and sanitize, we kill. When we introduce beneficial bugs into our gardens—nematodes into our soil—they are there to feed upon others. When we swat houseflies flat and crush that pesky mosquito that bites us…when we give our pets anti-parasitic medications…when we cut flowers and harvest vegetables… when we purchase lumber to build our homes to shelter our children…something dies.

SUCH IS LIFE. LIKE IT OR NOT, IT IS WHAT IT IS…

How can we live with ourselves in the face of all this carnage? That is where our cherished degrees come to life. We have created degrees of acceptability that, coupled with our denial of the facts, leave us with something we can comfortably digest. We find our comfort zone, our acceptable level of denial, and in typical predatory fashion, we look at those not like us, those who make us uncomfortable, and we attack them for *their* predatory tastes.

Do you feel inclined to disagree? Consider how disgusting we find the sight and smell of the result of our personal consumption. When will be the right time to get over ourselves? We all consume. That means we all kill. Is this a fact of life?

We all can grasp the idea of inspiration. That means we are inspired to great love and loyalty to our family, our nation, our universe, our higher power. Is this a fact of life?

We all have the capacity to accept what is. We are free to accept or resist it. Is this a fact of life?

It seems that accepting *what is a fact of life* at an elemental level would allow us to establish common ground, where inspiration is not denied but is as universally accepted as the building block of the elements that compose us. We would then agree that those same elements came to life in the footsteps of the dinosaurs and settled in the bones of the young soldiers who lost their lives in the battles of Hastings and Culloden and Passchendaele, whose life blood blended on the beaches of Normandy and then showed up in the young sapling that grew on the shores of the St. John River, only to be swept away by its flooding, its elements leaching into the water that slaked the thirst of the honeybee on its way upriver in order to pollinate your prized peony rose, passing in its way to present itself in the fleas of a thousand cattle that find their way into the best rib eye you have ever tasted, only to reveal itself with subtle elegance in the trusting eyes of your newborn child.

To deny our need to consume is insanity. To apologize for consuming is to deny life itself. To deny life saps every instant of its joy and strips away its meaning and purpose. It is, indeed, the death we so vigorously deny.

Take heart. We are these things, but we are so much more than these things.

> God sleeps in the minerals, awakens in plants, walks in animals, and thinks in man. —Arthur Young

We understand that we are more than the sum of this organism we inhabit, more than the process of our consumption. We are an organic compilation of elements, yes, but *through* our flowing synergistic expression, we realize inspiration.

In the words of the 14th Dalai Lama:

"IF YOU CAN, HELP OTHERS; IF YOU CANNOT DO THAT, AT LEAST DO NOT HARM THEM."

Why did we come to life? To what end will we find ourselves as we hurtle through space on this third rock from the sun? Life is always presenting us with the answers. Whatever we decide it is, it offers no apologies for its existence.

A Constant Traveler Reminder:
CONSCIOUS CONSUMPTION

Consider how you can become a more elegant, conscious consumer by reducing the waste generated by your daily practices.

Natural Resources waste. Something as simple as which toilet tissue you buy can have a significant impact. Which companies use old-growth forest to make your toilet tissue? This consideration takes on another level of environmental damage when we consider how often we purchase tissue rolls made from old-growth forest wrapped in plastic.

Plastic waste. How much of the plastic that you regularly toss into the recycling bin actually gets recycled? It is not enough to recycle, as conscious consumers we must rethink our voracious consumption and avoid buying plastic in the first place.

Water waste. How much potable water are we using when we take an extra-long shower? When we don't have a full load in our clothes washer? Every time we flush? Consider the environmental benefits of purchasing a low-flow toilet. Make sure your toilet doesn't waste water by constantly running. These measures will save on your water bill, as well as conserve potable water.

Food waste. It has been estimated that between 30 and 40 percent of the food supply goes to waste each year. According to the Commission for Environmental Cooperation (CEC), North Americans (USA, Canada, and Mexico) waste approximately 168 million tons of food per year. It is important to do the research that has the potential to save you hundreds of dollars in grocery costs. It pays to make a meal plan and buy only what you need, to bring leftovers home from a restaurant, to compost where you can, and to share food with others.

Energy waste. Be mindful of transportation fuel costs, household lights, TV, thermostat settings, leaving the computer on, etc. Be especially mindful of holiday displays that take energy to run. For example, as a nation, our Christmas lights can use more energy than *entire countries* use in a year. Impact your pocketbook as well as the environment in a positive way with new alternative energy solutions, and by using energy-efficient lighting.

We contribute to the health of our planet every day when we choose to use water filters, refillable drinking containers, and reusable shopping bags. Here are some examples that will not only generate less waste, but will send a message to manufacturers that we don't need more in the future:

Make eco-friendly packaging part of your purchasing decision. How can we reduce, reuse, or recycle the items we choose to buy? For example, avoid Styrofoam, plastic wrapped in plastic, disposable eating utensils, single-use straws, beverage bottles and cups, and plastic

(continued)

bags. Cloth shopping bags are not only strong, they can be washed and used for years. Form the habit of taking them with you into grocery stores and shopping malls. If you forget them, do not accept a plastic bag.

Purchase ethically sourced products from companies who contribute to the well-being of the planet. Look for those cosmetics and household products that are good for the environment and are not tested on animals. Buy clothing made of quality, organic materials that do not contribute to global GHG emissions, child labor, and human slavery. Another great option is to "rescue" clothing from secondhand and consignment stores. Otherwise, this clothing will end up in our local landfills.

Plan a meatless breakfast, lunch, and dinner one day per week. This will reduce your carbon footprint, reduce animal cruelty, and contribute to your personal health as well as the health of our planet.

Find elegant, creative ways to rethink the holidays. You can repurpose holiday greeting cards, flyers, brochures, novelties, gifts/wrapping paper, and avoid single-use decorations with the environment in mind. What would be the best possible choices for gift giving and filling treat bags?

Bravo! You have now become part of the solution! Your neighbors, the critters with whom we share this land, but most especially *your children and your children's children* will be better off because of you.

6

An Elegant Mind Does Not Resist Experience.

It discovers the meaning in each experience and acts with this knowledge in mind.

It's a fact of life. Sometimes you succeed and sometimes you fail. Call it growth. From your earliest memory to your last breath, you will grow in one way or another. You will win sometimes. You will fail sometimes. The secret to growing in a positive direction and learning something from each setback is how you respond to the failure. How can you value each experience? How can you find meaning in defeat?

LIVE. LEARN. GROW WISER.

An elegant loss becomes as honorable as an elegant win when you ask:

What can I gain from this? How can I grow stronger?

How can I become more resilient, act with more courage, become more focused?

How can I deepen my faith in my abilities? In my worthiness?

In what ways can I become more creative? More compassionate?

33

How can I become wiser?

Once you apply what you've learned—then, *you win every time*. Wisdom is realizing the value of experience.

WHY
What is it? What is wrong?
I've been asking this for so long!
There are so many things that I don't understand
So many moments that slip through my hands…
Like water—I can't hold the thing,
yet my hands seem to never be dry.
Can someone please answer me, why?
What is that sound? Was it there all along?
Is that music I hear in the words of a song,
or is it my tears in a heartbroken dream?
I keep looking behind for the answer, it seems…
Do I love those old words,
repurposed, well-worn,
because they conform
to my vision of what used to be?
When there's nothing left back there of me?
Why is this, what it is?
Why can I not be, not believe,
not accept what I am?
Why am I always in need
when I don't want to be?
Can I have it my way every once in a while
without reparation and guilt?
Do I have to keep sifting through filth?

—PDT

Life without experience is death. Experience brings with it the potential for wisdom. To discover the meaning of an experience, it is necessary to approach it with an attitude of welcome and the intention to gain something worthwhile from it.

THE WORLD DOES NOT CONFORM TO YOUR VERSION OF WHAT IS BECAUSE THE WORLD DOES NOT CONFORM TO YOUR VERSION OF WHAT IS...

It is just that simple. It is a waste of energy to fight with reality. Resisting experience does not change it. Resistance changes you—it makes you harder to change.

A Constant Traveler Reminder:
BECOME AN ELEGANT LOSER

Are you gracious in defeat?
Can you take the best of this experience, learn from it, and grow?
How are you better for this defeat?
Will you let this defeat defeat you?

We need to remember that circumstances don't make a person, they reveal a person.
—Emma Jameson

7

An Elegant Mind Is Grateful
That It Knows More Than It Did Yesterday...

...and joyful because it knows less
than it will tomorrow.

Gratitude opens minds, eyes, and hearts to the timeless state of receptivity. It welcomes and accepts those everyday miracles that are the fruits of gratefulness. A grateful mind understands that discovery is its most effective use of time.

Giving thanks is grace for you.
Its grace extends to others too.
Express your love and change your brain.
This sets the stage for more of the same.

ANTICIPATED WITH THE WIDE-EYED INNOCENCE OF
A CHILD DISCOVERING ITS WORLD, HOW COULD
TOMORROW BE ANYTHING BUT JOYFUL?

WOW! (WORDS OF WISDOM)

Knowing means *done in full awareness or consciousness.* What is awareness or consciousness? We can discuss the concept. Others can explain it. But if knowing is what we are, what can we truly say we know? That is humbling. Then we must admit what we really know for sure.

What is knowledge? Is it an intellectual acuity? A comprehension of the facts? Or is it a perception, a familiarity gained through experience of a fact or situation?

How do we express what we know? Is it enough that we can spout theory, or is it through practical application that we prove that which we know?

WE LIVE OUR LIVES FROM WHAT
WE KNOW FOR SURE...

This is a neutral statement about life. It does not make what we know true—*it makes it true for us.* And what we know for sure may or may not be life-promoting. We learn, assimilate, and apply knowledge to our life. Our life reflects what we know for sure now. We can be very smug and pious about it. To examine what we know for sure in a comprehensive manner, we must examine both positive and negative aspects.

When I understand the basics that enhance and promote life, I become them; they become me.

If I know patience, I am patient.
If I know trust, I am trusting and trustworthy.
If I know kindness, I am kind.
If I know compassion, I am compassionate.

WHAT DO WE KNOW FOR SURE?

Traditionally we consider knowledge as that which we accumulate. With an accumulation of the negative, we become a knowledgeable yet evil mastermind. With an accumulation of the positive, we become wise. If I understand the basics that threaten and destroy life, I become them; they become me.

If I know fear, I am fearful.
If I know survival of the fittest, I am competition.
If I know my enemy, I am my enemy.

I would like to offer another perspective: *What if being wise is not a matter of accumulation but of relinquishment?* Perhaps wisdom is found in releasing the value we place on concepts, beliefs, and ideals as well as our thoughts on competition and consequences. Consider the following statement that refers to a revelatory WOW! experience:

ONCE WE KNOW, WE CANNOT NOT KNOW...

It is like time stands still. We say we feel a jolt of inspiration, of life-changing understanding that is generally considered as being "given" to us from somewhere else. What if it isn't? What if it does not come from anywhere? What if it was there all along, and the juggernaut we call revelation had enough energy to halt the chatter and punch a pinhole in the box, releasing our inspiration and allowing us to "think outside the box"?

Perhaps we suffer so deeply because we think small and are distracted by fear. You can label this small box "me" if you so desire. We will never know that we are inside a box if we cling to it. Whatever its name, it keeps me small and scared. I am its servant—unless I embrace creativity. Creativity brings the WOW! moments. It is vital.

We are always learning, regardless of how we conceptualize it or attempt to compartmentalize it. Think about the term *concept*. It is a general notion, a symbolic representation of a coagulation of thought used to form our perceptions into something communicate-able. And we compartmentalize our concepts. It is human nature to attempt to categorize and label each aspect of life, to put them into sturdy, solidly built boxes. This we find comfortable and safe.

To the discerning student, all education is useful education. *The wise student wastes nothing.* This gratitude is manifested by the student applying what they have learned in life to grow and evolve. They understand that their best life will be achieved not only through surviving events (this is a transition period) but by using this to overcome and become stronger—to become a *thriver.* They differentiate the things they know from the things they *believe they know* by the following criterion: They consciously live what they know for sure.

A Constant Traveler Reminder:
WALKING THE TALK

What do you know for sure? Can you substitute the word *live* for the word *know* in your statements?

8

An Elegant Mind Realizes That an Open Heart Lets in More Sunlight.

It focuses on the sunlight and not the flecks of dust the sunlight exposes.

There is incredible beauty in the world, and very little of it is flawless. However, it can be perfect to us if we choose to see it that way.

THE SPECKS OF DUST WE NOTICE IN THE SUN'S RAYS ALSO CREATE ITS MOST SPECTACULAR SUNSETS...

There is a time to focus on details, most certainly, but there is a yin for every yang. The elegant mind knows when to lean back and enjoy life just as it is.

Perfectionism is just a delay logic fancied up to look respectable.
—Brendon Burchard

Words are symbols for thoughts, which are also symbols that represent something deeper—the creative wellspring from which all thoughts spring. Thoughts can be life-promoting or destructive. Understand that the word *perfection* is a human construct. It is your attempt to capture with words that which eludes capture. You have an idea, you verbalize it and communicate it, and because much of your conditioning and communicative ability is gained in your formative years, delivered by those you depended upon for survival, you agreed. It is part of the human condition.

Words have extraordinary power whether driven through the energy of love or through the energy of fear. Perfection seems to hold an extraordinary power over us; it is deeply embedded in our thought system. I cannot suspend your caring about something so deeply embedded. My words, most likely, will not scratch the surface of your vision of perfection. The only person who can determine how to get to the bottom of this dilemma is you.

However, I can offer you another perspective: *Perfection*, as the dictionary defines it, is the state of being faultless, flawless, or free of defects.

Who or what suggests that you are at fault? *Realize that whatever it is, you fear it.*

Who or what contends that you are flawed? *Understand that whatever it is, you fear it.*

Why would you believe yourself to be defective? *This is an important key to uncovering why you are fearful, including your fear of being imperfect.* I would suggest that you have agreed to this ideal, spent most of your life constructing a vision that is beyond you, and are now in despair because you realize you are struggling and can never attain this vision.

You have become your own jailer and torturer. Realize that your vision has made you driven, unhappy, and reliant upon others (or another) for approval, desperate for some form of peace. This vision can strip you of your personal power and take over your life if you agree with it.

A Constant Traveler Reminder:
NATURE BATHING

It is important to gain perspective and allow your mind to relax into the moment.

Take a nature bath today—go on a nature walk. Walk through the forest or closest park. Sit by the water and listen to the waves. Watch the squirrels or birds. No phones, no music. Listen to the sounds of nature for a half hour or more.

9

An Elegant Mind Knows It Is Always the Right Time to Begin Again.

Dear Today,

It's me again. Wanted you to know that you are on my mind.

I don't say this nearly enough, and I am making a pledge right here and now to have these little chats with you a lot more, okay?

Okay. Well, here goes.

Today, I appreciate you. My life would be nothing without you. I mean, what would I be without you? In what would I move and have my being if not you? I know the answer to that one well enough. I wouldn't even be hanging out with you now, would I? Suffice to say, I get it. You and I are all I have, really. And Today, I sure am grateful for your company.

You give so much of yourself, always there when I need you. Thanks for showing up, bud! Your generosity is boundless! I do try to be like you and share my time in the same way that you share yours—to always keep your example in mind—but I get distracted sometimes. And I feel crappy when that happens, come to think of it.

But you've taught me how useless it is to waste our one-on-one time feeling crappy about other days when I have YOU right here, right now, and I know I am beginning to sound like a broken record, with these words stuck on repeat, but *thanks again* for that lesson.

Come to think of it, I guess a person could do a lot worse than to have "THANK YOU" stuck on repeat, right?

I've made a list of outstanding things that I have to do, Today. I've looked at my list and considered the worthiness of each item, just like you've taught me to do. I don't want to take away from our quality time together. I know your time is valuable, and there may be a lot less of it—with me in it, I mean—than I would like to imagine. Or there may be plenty of time. But there is never enough time to piddle any of it away, right? Who knows how much time we really do have together? Not me, and you keep reminding me, whispering in my ear, that right here, right now, "You got me, babe. All of me."

I know, and it's cool, and I love ya, ya know, with everything I've got. Because Today, you're my world.

You know that yesterday I was sad. Someone I loved more than life died. Actually, more than one someone… and yesterday I wasn't feeling too good about myself. I was struggling. It was like someone sneaked up behind me and threw a soggy, woolen, king-size blanket over me, and I couldn't get it off quickly enough, and I fell down. It felt like I was onstage in a circus tent, and the show was about to start, and the glaring spotlight was always on me, and I couldn't seem to remember my lines, but I couldn't forget them either. And I knew that you had a new script waiting for me in the wings, but my hands were sweaty and sticky from the one I had from yesterday. I couldn't seem to drop it. But Today, you showed me how to look at my hands, see what I was holding onto, and simply let that worn-out old rag of a script go. Let it fall to the ground. I was so ready.

I know, you keep reminding me, and keep it up, please. I like that you are always fresh and new and that every time I open my eyes I find myself on this side of the grass once again. Here with you.

And if you would be so kind, please tell me once again about how yesterday died and how I should leave it in the land of the dead and that I can't truly live with you while still dragging it along, Today. Please explain why I should travel lightly and keep my head up and flash the world a little grin every once in a while. I want to show the folks just what a darling you are—a sweetheart, a superstar. How proud I am to be with you!

And gently remind me that I cannot really get to know you if I don't share you and remind everyone that you love hanging out with every person alive, Today, and that they have exactly what you and I have together. Why I should shout it out through my eyes, my hands, my words that YOU ROCK! And urge them to seize you, this once-in-a-lifetime opportunity!

I have a wish on my list for you, Today. I would like to offer all of my friends and the friends that I haven't met yet my wish for their best day ever, and that they find the motivation and energy to celebrate each passing second as it takes them deeper into their very best life.

And for those who find themselves on the battleground, wounded and alone, may they feel your resolve, your optimism, your resilience. As long as they have breath, they will once again open their eyes and find you here, fresh and new, every morning.

And will you please extend my love to those with whom we will part company, Today? Because we understand that the way of all things is to be stripped of all things, and that we have only so much time together.

Today, this moment, right now, you are the best I will ever know. I'm so happy you are in my life, and I'm excited to see where you're taking me!

Here's my to-do list: No. 1, remember that every day I wake up on this side of the grass is a beautiful day!

Done!

Take care, my friend. We'll talk again really soon.

A Constant Traveler Reminder
TAKE ACTION

Check your life-goals list. Considering that tomorrow never comes, what can you do today instead of choosing to put off until tomorrow?

You don't have a life-goals list? Now is the perfect time to create one.

10

An Elegant Mind Recognizes That to Not Choose Is to Choose Nonetheless.

STONE SHOES

I need new shoes. The old ones have lost their support and are beginning to hurt my feet. And I have picked up stones along the way. The soles seemed to be filling with stones that gather in the cracks and holes. I am getting tired of having to dig them out.

So, today I went to the shoe store.

I've seen the advertisements on TV and dreamed of the feel of new shoes—those really nice ones made of the finest material, gossamer light, unbroken-in by any other feet. For months now I've thought of at least *stopping by* the shoe store just to look, but for some reason I didn't.

I don't want to seem like a vain shoe person, but on the other hand I don't want to hang onto old, beat-up shoes too long due to pure stubbornness.

However, I must admit that these old ones feel like me. They smell like me. *They are still good.*

Today I was feeling adventurous…I decided it was the day I wouldn't just walk on by. I didn't think about it, I just veered to the left and before I knew it, I was inside.

It was cool and quiet in this store. The walls were painted a deep rich green. Vague music…might have been Rosemary Clooney or even Norah Jones…was playing soft and smooth, mingling with the gleaming glass cabinets and polished dark wood shelves.

The cobbler was sitting behind an antique workbench, a soft green lamp illuminating his work. He greeted me with a smile-over-glasses and then went back to the task at hand. It seemed this cobbler was used to people popping in to look at new shoes.

Tap, tap, tap—each nail driven with the expert side of a slender silver file…creating shoes well heeled, skillfully and lovingly constructed to stand the test of time.

These were custom-made footwear. Quality leather. Fine stitching. *Soles with no holes.*

I felt a surge of excitement. Impulsively I took off my shoes and stood on the cobbler's cool, elegantly polished, gleaming plank floor.

The cobbler could see my bare feet on his fine floor. It made me feel strange.

I kept my eyes down, looking at my toes. My old shoes were right there, still warm from the heat of me. I tried to ignore the slight smell of my stinky toes, but I couldn't. And I didn't want to gross up this fine store.

I could see the stones peeking up from the bottom, through my still untied laces. I had to smile. Some of those stones felt like friends. They were like my pet rocks, their rough edges worn comfortable.

Just like old memories.

Feeling silly one day, I had named my favorite rock, Regret.

"Rock on!" I thought. What can ya' do but laugh about it, right? The person who doesn't take their laughter with a splash of wry is a sorry person indeed.

I eyed my shoes with pride. They may be scuffed and pedestrian...*ordinary*...but they were solid. They could still kick ass.

I was sure that the elegant patrons of this store would never kick ass. They would have a servant do it for them. I felt the chill of the cool polished floor creeping up my legs. It made me shiver. I didn't belong in this fine store. Perhaps this was not the right time to buy new shoes. And this place was very expensive, I must add...

"Too dear," as my elderly grandfather used to say.

Some podiatrists prescribe shoes with pressure points in the soles to enhance health. I wonder if that is what my old shoes are doing for me—they do rub my feet as I walk.

I could feel the vague beginnings of that familiar ache, the burn that was not yet pain. It happens if I stand for too long barefoot on a flat, smooth floor. Or, *shoes on or off*...if I stand too long in one place.

"My feet are complaining," I like to explain with a sheepish grin. I blame it on *Arthur*, grandfather's name for arthritis. *Arthur's a bad actor today*...he used to joke as he rubbed his sore feet. My Pop was silly too.

The cobbler caught my eye. "Just finished a really nice pair," he said and smiled, "Try these."

He offered me the *most lovely* shoes I think I have ever seen! My eyes caressed their fine lines, softly polished by an expert hand.

His best, I could tell by the craftsman's pride in his eyes.

I really loved the color! I took them gently in my hands. They were feather light and I was certain they were my size.

"Try them on," the cobbler urged.

I wasn't sure...new shoes always chafe at first. And they are always too tight. And I hadn't brought any socks with me—I couldn't wear those gross little footlets that stores provide to their customers. I could never be certain that they weren't used.

I could tell by the cobbler's tone that he didn't think I was going to try them. Nah, he knew what I was thinking...*those shoes were too rich for my blood.*

Who did he think he was, anyway?

I hesitated, but then handed them back to the cobbler. I put on my shoes.

"Maybe another day," I said.

My hand was already on the door.

Many times, we choose one thing over another, putting the fine dreams that take time and energy to accomplish aside in order to live what seems like a comfortable life.

How many of us voluntarily gave up on our dreams, choosing to play it safe and take it easy instead? Even if it means feeling that we are living someone else's dream? Or nightmare?

It may be uncomfortable to leave what we have come to know as safety, even if it is deathly boring. Even if we must admit that it sucks. Even if it is so "hard on the head" that we don't know which way is up most of the time. Even if, when we look back at the past year, the past five years, the past 10 years... all that we see is our younger selves struggling in the mire.

Setting off into the unknown is risky. If we choose door A, we may suffer. If we choose door B, we may suffer. If we choose door C, we may suffer. *However, if we don't choose any door at all, choosing instead to stay where we are with what we know, we will inevitably suffer the loss of our power to choose. Not choosing is a choice as well, only with this choice we hand over our power...and the direction of our precious lives…to the whims of others.*

Living elegantly means to live with dignity and respect for our own abilities—those that have been realized and those yet unrealized—and taking steps toward creating our best life from that perspective. These steps are impossible to accomplish if we insist on thinking like the person in the story, wearing shoes full of holes just because we are used to them.

A Constant Traveler Reminder:
ENGAGE IN SERIOUS PLAY

*When was the last time you did something for
the first time?* —John C. Maxwell

Learn to seriously play by taking yourself out on an adventure! Take on a new physical exercise! Mount an expedition! Here are a few suggestions:
- Biking
- Archery
- Jogging
- Dancing (hip-hop, jazz, belly dancing, etc.)
- Yoga
- Resistance training
- Skiing
- Snowshoeing
- Tennis
- Badminton
- Or...try a different shoe store!

*Our suffering doesn't come from life being unfair
but from our disagreement with it.*

11

An Elegant Mind Accepts
That Life Is Change.

An integrated ecosystem is an elegant demonstration of flowing coherence. It flourishes. It is a synergistic blend of diverse functions that adapts and changes with circumstances, and restructures according to new information and experience. This statement can be applied to a successful ecosystem.

To thrive is life's highest expression of change. Adaptation is the expression of a life designed to thrive...

Change is an integral part of its design. Change is introduction. It is adaptation and assimilation. Without this influx, the system would stagnate. Change renders that impossible. When a previously unknown element is introduced into an ecosystem, it changes the system by interrupting the natural flow. Consequently, following its first nature, the system adapts.

The process of adaptation prompts one of the following:

• **The entire system becomes more diverse and adaptable.** It is strengthened and enhanced by this element. Consequently, the system achieves a new balance.

• **The system does not support this element. It fails to integrate.** In time the system returns to a balance very similar to its original state but with one exception: the experience or new information provided by the attempted integration.

• **The system, overwhelmed by this new element, fails to integrate it.** Established boundaries cannot be sustained, and the entire ecosystem disintegrates.

However, change is endless. Regardless of whether this system thrives or collapses, the consequences of this interaction lead to a result and, inevitably, a new order. From this perspective, we reframe what we regard as the capricious nature of change.

CROW TREE
On upmost tip of least,
most barren branch
of this most common,
threadbare tree
at roadway's side,
a crow sits.

Its dark-night plumage
punctuates the sky,
ripe with shadows,
insolence, and sheen.

From where I sit and roll along,
content to ride this solid earth,
the tendril branch it grasps
is foreign ground.

A precarious perch, indeed.

What goings-on its sharp eyes see,
reflecting sun and cloudy skies,
asphalt and afterthoughts...
amid the Go! Go! Go! of every man
and me?

We scurry on, oblivious and
most ignorant to
what lies below,
our tender underbelly exposed
by the hapless creature
who, in one
time-sharp moment,
zigged
instead of
zagged.

While in its bloated,
sun-drenched state
it lies,
exposing rot and loss and pain,
and such...
as we envision death.

From where it sits, the crow reflects
upon its sharpened lens,
its visions of
both death in life...
and life in death.

Which one sees more clearly, friend?
—PDT

The foundational energetic flux we call change is constant. Nothing interrupts its essential state. The closest we can come to describe this constant is by its expression. This may not be its most pure expression; this is where descriptors fall short, as they are limited by the boundaries of the human mind. You cannot realize it; you can only realize its manifestations. You cannot anticipate or control its manifestations; you can only adapt to them. This possibility catapults you into a vast and deeply frightening expanse.

Change is. It may or it may not promote life. This is the aspect of change that terrifies human beings. Regardless, it remains unchanged by your fearful response to what is a threat to life. You attempt to resist change, but it remains, neither energized nor de-energized by your resistance. *Only you are.*

In this regard, life can be considered an ecosystem. This ecosystem is the basic framework that supports life and death. You move through life from birth to death, immersed in its flow, very much like a person paddling a kayak.

To support life as you know it, you are presented with the following options:

- **You can paddle with the stream**—thereby exerting minimal effort to achieve maximum reward.
- **You can paddle against the stream**—exerting maximum effort and realizing minimum reward.
- **You can stop paddling**—this translates to giving in to the current. Extrinsic forces dictate your course.

Regardless, the stream takes you…

Consider this scene as an observer, viewing it from above the ecosystem:

From far above, the three elements (the paddler, the kayak, and the ecosystem) blend and flow as one. On the water (the human level), you can understand yourself as the new element—the kayaker. You are following the stream. From this perspective, you make choices based upon the flow of the water and the obstructions in the stream. Conflict results in the mind that does not recognize where it fits into the whole—as the paddler, the kayak, and the ecosystem—because on a level beyond your current comprehension, you are composed of the elements by which the whole system originates. To accept this would mean accepting the natural flow of life and death.

You resist change because:

- You consider survival a triumph.
- You consider thriving a sustained, collaborative triumph.
- You consider death (failure to survive or thrive) the Ultimate Fail.

This perpetual resistance to change creates perpetual suffering. Change is, essentially, beyond all things.

A Constant Traveler Reminder
PRAYER PLANT EXERCISE

This is an exercise first presented in my book *Saving Your Own Life: Learning to Live Like You Are Dying.* Consider it a practice of mindful observation of each element in the process of growing a healthy, vibrant houseplant.

There is a lovely plant, indigenous to the Brazilian rainforest that has been named the prayer plant. It earned this name because of the way its leaves fold together at night—those observing it thought it looked like hands closing in prayer.

I have often thought of Mother Teresa as a person who not only lived a prayerful life but whose life was a living prayer. Her simple, practical, and dedicated effort to assist others has been deeply inspirational to the whole world. She was a gift to the planet.

I love being surrounded by growing things. It is a delight to observe people growing into their appreciation and awareness of their personal potential; a joy to assist others in the expansion of their minds and life experiences as I grow and expand into my own; to celebrate the profusion of life through nurturing actual plants in my home and garden.

Plants not only feed us and purify our air, but they also provide an aesthetic beauty that is defiant of words.

I have a prayer plant in my collection. It grows well but prefers a bit of attention—well-drained soil and full sunlight to thrive. Its leaves are a lovely soft green, and it grows thick and vigorous with a taste of fertilizer every second week or so.

Also, in my plant collection I have a very healthy potted heartleaf philodendron. As I watered it today, I saw that it has begun twining its way through a rustic iron tree that I placed next to it. Other shoots are reaching for the light and intertwining themselves with one another, some growing up as they also grow down, getting longer and longer. Each day, it seems, I discover another young heart unfolding at the end of each vine.

This plant reminds me of the elegant life of Mother Teresa...

Gratitude is prayer...

Depending on your approach to life, you could consider this (or any plant you desire) to be a "prayer" or "focus" plant. Watching your plant grow is the point of this exercise.

This plant is the symbol of your agreement to nurture your elegant mind. Each day, as you greet your morning, consider your plant's progress. Each time you water it and give it fertilizer, consider its growth. If it is not thriving in the spot where you put it, then consider why this is so. Does it have enough light (analogous to your open mind)? Does it have enough water or too much water (analogous to how you are doing in becoming comfortable with your thoughts)? Does it have enough fertilizer (analogous to feeding your mind with uplifting and inspiring material)?

Consider its roots. Strong roots equal a beautiful, vigorous plant. It is a physical demonstration of your compassionate focus on your growing awareness, an example of how your life can be a living prayer.   (continued)

It is also a source of contemplation by itself. Consider its beauty, how each leaf forms in precisely the right place, unbidden by anything except the simple elegance of it being exactly what it is. It springs forth from the soil with unencumbered gracefulness. Its lush, shining green leaves are indeed something colored beautiful.

The heartleaf philodendron is a spectacularly hardy plant. It can grow in most places in the home and thrives in a wide range of conditions. It is very easy to propagate (ask for a slip from a friend—it will root in water or even in moist soil) or easy to purchase, as they are generally cheap and plentiful in garden stores.

I urge you to get yourself a plant (possibly a philodendron or ivy, due to their vigorous, easily observable growth) and begin this nurturing practice today.

If the only prayer you ever say in your entire life is thank you, it will be enough.
—Meister Eckhart

12

An Elegant Mind Demonstrates That Kindness Is Natural.

Life is so very difficult. How can we be anything but kind?
—Jack Kornfield

It is as natural to feel kindness as it is to feel its opposite. If you haven't felt or shared kindness, it's not because you don't have that ability; you simply haven't experienced that side of you. If you do not feel kindness, you are not enjoying an aspect of your nature. You have no problem agreeing that hatred is learned behavior. What you have more trouble understanding is that *self-hatred* is also learned behavior.

THE NATURAL UNIVERSE

The natural world exists with respect. Up is only up with respect to down. In is only in with respect to out. Death is only death with respect to life. You believe what you are with respect to what you are not. *The common denominator is respect, meaning esteem, regard, or aspect.*

Respect is the key to understanding:

• That which is closed can be opened.

• That which moves can be stilled.

• That which engages in endless chatter can be silenced.

In those everyday moments when you feel unhappy, you are indulging in something *other than* kindness—toward yourself or toward others. Can you consider that you have formed this belief? Do you honor your belief more than you honor your life—so much that you dare not examine it?

This belief is your challenge. It has showed up in your life so you can feel the full spectrum of what it means to be human.

Consider others your mirror. It is not about their being unkind—it is about you letting go of your unkindness. It is not about blaming them or him or her or it for not being kind, but about letting go of your belief in being unworthy of being kind.

THE CHOICE TO WALK CREATES THE PATH AHEAD...

The choice to walk not only opens the door; it creates the door. This isn't fantasy—the human brain works this way. Over eons we have evolved to look for patterns and cues in our immediate environment and tune out extraneous information. Watch the television show *Brain Games* for a demonstration. It is how magicians do what they do. It isn't supernatural—it is entirely natural, predictable, and measurable. That is why a magician's tricks work every time.

A person doesn't have to be a magician or understand magic tricks to understand what principles and science are being used to create them. You trick yourself into believing the good, the bad, and the ugly. If you believe this, then you can also choose what you use to create your best life.

Consider carefully where you place your attention and your focus. Choose unrelenting kindness and observe what is reflected back to you.

If it's natural to kill, how come men have to go into training to learn how? —Joan Baez

A Constant Traveler Reminder:
KISS NOT CURSE

How do you use the time you spend standing in line? It is not always easy, but this *training ground is priceless*. Standing in line, like any aspect of your day, offers you a unique opportunity, if you choose to look at it that way.

With a little practice, you can use standing in line as an automatic reminder to live in *the gap*—that is, the space where you have the presence of mind to relax and remember that *losing your cool is a choice*. Nothing or no one has the power to draw you out of this space, *but you can lose it*.

Use the time when you are standing in line to become more aware of your feelings, your surroundings, and other people. Smile when you catch someone's eye and practice doing **everything gently**—being deliberate with every thought, word, and action.

Send others good vibes—it is a non-judgmental exercise I call **Kiss Not Curse**. Send them goodwill wrapped in a psychic blessing!

It's all sacred ground or nothing is sacred ground.
It's all sacred ground if you choose to think of it that way.

13

An Elegant Mind Knows That Kindness Is the Key to Lasting Happiness.

It demonstrates that life changes to happy
when we are being kind.

The *English Oxford Dictionary* defines *kindness* as the quality of being friendly, generous, and considerate. *Merriam-Webster,* defines *kindness* as the quality or state of *being* gentle and considerate. In psychology, the definition of happiness is an emotional state of well-being that can be defined by positive or pleasant emotions ranging from contentment to intense joy.

What if kindness is happiness? What if the feeling we get when we are being kind is what happiness feels like? Maybe we have misconstrued happiness for some other feeling, some transient pleasure that it is not.

Kindness is a state of mind. It is also an action. It is also an elegant lifestyle.

KINDNESS IS WHAT HAPPINESS FEELS LIKE.

A Constant Traveler Reminder:
THE NEW NORMAL

Kindness is an action word. Freely given and priceless to receive, kindness is a gift that happily keeps on giving.

Overnight, it seems, our world has been catapulted into a new frontier. Life is changing but it can change for the better.

FLOWER CHILDREN

I live on a rural country road. During the period of physical distancing my husband and I walked a lot. One day we began to see something colored beautiful along the way...small stones painted with hearts and flowers, and kind, uplifting words like, *I have your back.* and *Keep your chin up.*

Some neighborhood children had painted them and put them on the side of the road, in places where everyone who walked could enjoy them.

Each time I go out I look for them. Sometimes they are moved. Sometimes there are new stones there to greet me.

Each time I see one of these brightly painted stones, I smile. And I believe in the resiliency of humanity...and the bright-eyed optimism of a new generation...even more deeply. It truly makes me happy! I wish to protect and preserve this precious resource.

First printed by Anne Hebert on placemat in Sausalito, California, the phrase "practice random kindness and senseless acts of beauty" has become part of our everyday, *normal*, language.

Can random acts of kindness and senseless acts of beauty lead to happiness? Of course, they can! But we must, as one of the stones say, *Believe*.

As soon as possible, make kindness *your new normal*.

Support small, local businesses.

Pick up groceries for an elderly neighbor.

Contribute to your local food bank or community kitchen.

Visit an elderly resident in a nursing home who has no relatives.

Compliment a great waiter or waitress to their manager.

Embrace new technology. Connect regularly with friends and family online.

Always say Yes! and contribute whenever a charity comes into your awareness.

Buy a gift for a kid who is in foster care.

Put a quarter in an expired parking meter.

Run or walk for a charitable cause.

When you go for a walk, take a bag, and pick up as much trash as the bag will hold

Lead with your hand
Lead with your heart
Lead with your welcome
Lead with your heart...

14

An Elegant Mind Offers Peace through Ordinary Day-to-Day Living.

It acknowledges that what it shares with the world returns in kind.

There is no path to peace. Peace is the path.
—Gandhi

You use the word *peace* a lot, but have you really considered what peace is? Sometimes it is easier to understand peace by what it is not, but that does not give you its definition; it provides you with a vision of its antithesis. You resist that image, and by doing so you energize the very thing you do not want. However, you can use this negation. When you allow your rejection to strip away that which peace is not, *you will be left with what it is.*

Everything, including peace in your world, begins with you. How can you know peace if you are not peaceful? Peace is a state of being, an aspect of the collective mind that you share with others. There are many wonderful demonstrations of peace in our world. Why is it that you don't recognize them?

71

Mother Teresa showed you that "peace begins with a smile." In his classic book of the same name, Buddhist master Thich Nhat Hanh teaches that *Peace Is Every Step.* It is simple.

The elegant mind offers peace with each thought, each breath, and each gesture. It is present in every moment of its ordinary day. It looks, curiously, like acceptance.

A Constant Traveler Reminder:
LIVING PEACE

Most would agree that just because someone offers you something doesn't mean you have to take it. With this in mind, you have a choice whether to "take" offense. Follow Mother Teresa's example. Read and learn from the wisdom of Thich Nhat Hanh:

Give peace. That is how you will recognize it.
Live peace. That is how you know it.

Gratefully offer peace to everyone you meet today.

15

An Elegant Mind Creates Goals and Objectives...

...and quietly works toward achieving them.

Just stand, that's all.
Keep your eyes on the prize and stand up tall.
Don't look down, there's nothing down there on the ground.
Don't just survive—know for real you're alive. You're alive!

GIVE 'ER!

There is a saying in my part of the world for when we want to encourage someone to do something. We say, "Give 'er!" It means "Give it your best!" or "Go for it!" When someone has given their best effort, an observer may say, "He has given 'er!"

Vision and effort are realized in the present moment. Feeling energetic is powerful. Enthusiasm is power. That's what given 'er is all about!

While working toward your goal, it is good to keep in mind that successful people do everything they can to achieve, *espe-*

cially the things that unsuccessful people won't do. They know that patience is the key that opens the door to future success, and they keep in mind that discontent and frustration have sabotaged many a worthy goal. They have reframed failure by considering it the process of trial and error. Trial and error are aspects of achievement, and failure in one area leads them away from what does not work.

As an infant you learned by taking baby steps. Can you accept learning by baby steps now? No matter how deeply you desire it, would you take a two-year-old to a graduate class in rocket science and expect them to function? Preparation takes time.

Do the work and proceed with confidence. Expect opportunities to show up when (and where) you least expect them.

THOSE WHO SAY IT CAN'T BE DONE CAN DO ONE
THING: THEY CAN MOVE OUT OF THE WAY OF
THOSE DOING IT...

A Constant Traveler Reminder:
KAIZEN

There is a practice in Japanese culture called *kaizen*. It is the process of making small improvements, taking baby steps toward a goal. Improvements using this technique can begin with the smallest action that requires very little effort. Make the steps so small you cannot fail!

Have a goal in mind? Ask yourself, What small step can I take right now? If that feels overwhelming, then make it a smaller step.

Example: You have been putting off cleaning your messy closet. For some reason it feels overwhelming, and you have been procrastinating. Set your goal to fold one item. That's it. Each time you visit your closet, fold one item. With this continuous progress, it won't be long until you see real-life results. Research has proven that this technique works.

Low-key change helps the human mind circumnavigate the fear that blocks success and creativity. —Robert Maurer

There is another upside to *kaizen* practice besides having a clean closet—this process includes rewards!

TINY DELIGHTS!

Think of a small indulgence that gives you pleasure. It can be a favorite restaurant, a movie, a walk, a quiet bath,
(continued)

a massage, or a phone call with an old friend. No reward is too small to utilize in this way.

There are those who indulge in little treats—but use these carefully. For example: If you love almonds and would like to incorporate them into your diet, place a dish on your dresser, and indulge in one every time you fold a piece of clothing in your closet. This is a small, healthy reward that allows you to celebrate this small goal!

On the other hand, you must be very cautious if you use food as your reward. This process may provide enough (or too many) tiny delights so that you overindulge. We all know the risks of overeating and drinking. If you are on a calorie-restricted diet or feel you cannot afford the extra calories, be health-minded when rewarding yourself.

Another option could be to ask a friend or loved one to give you a hug in celebration of your goal. If you live alone, you could have a great song that you love ready, and hit play!

This process is based on solid science. What is happening here is that you are training your brain to not go into fear mode. Fear of failure causes procrastination and leads to feeling overwhelmed. By taking small steps that guarantee success, you are reinforcing the actions that lead to the good stuff. You are, slowly and surely, forming a good habit.

One small, simple step can be to create a list of tiny delights with which you can reward yourself after you accomplish your small goals.

Create a Happiness Playlist consisting of 10 songs that make you smile and wanna get your groove on—

songs you can access anytime you want to give yourself a reward. You can see my Happiness Playlist below. I realize everyone has their own taste in music and there are certain songs that make your heart smile any time anywhere. Don't worry if others think your songs are corny or too sweet. They are your songs that sing to you and celebrate your happiness. Have fun with it!

For more information on the technique of *kaizen*, check out *One Small Step Can Change Your Life: The Kaizen Way* by Robert Maurer, Ph.D.

PAULA'S HAPPINESS PLAYLIST

"Happy" by Pharrell Williams

"Don't Worry Be Happy" by Bobby McFerrin

"Soak Up the Sun" by Sheryl Crow

"Bring the Funk" by Parliament Funkadelic

"Uptown Funk" by Mark Ronson, featuring Bruno Mars

"I Gotta Feeling" by the Black Eyed Peas

"The Fox (What Does the Fox Say?)" by Ylvis

"Good to Be Alive (Hallelujah)" by Andy Grammer

"Can't Stop the Feeling!" by Justin Timberlake

"Stompa" by Serena Ryder

"Born This Way" by Lady Gaga

16

An Elegant Mind Does Its Best Each Day
Without Comparing Itself to Others.

If you are doing your best, be happy. If another is doing their best, be happy for them. If the reason you strive to achieve is to best someone else, is this what's best for you?

Judging changes my best into my bad. Who takes responsibility? ME! It is my experience.

WILL THE CEMETERY BE THE REPOSITORY
FOR YOUR DREAMS?

Many people reach the end of their lives with regrets— regrets about relationships, about their personal contributions, their dreams and achievements and their failures.

Consider dreams life goals. This takes them out of the realm of imagination (where all dreams and goals are created) and gives them substance. It makes them achievable.

It has been noted that the biggest regret of those at the end of their lives is that they hadn't lived in a fierce manner—more deeply, more courageously—like the man or woman whose life goals were imagined when they were younger, before the choices they made took them on an entirely different path, decisions that led away from those wonderful goals.

It is wise to consider that every choice you make alters the direction of your life. Each one alters your personal timeline significantly. It is also wise to look at your personal predilection for anticipating obstacles and toward lethargy, and to work toward resolving these to the best of your ability. This takes constant work, even for the people who realize their life goals—those who are living them now. They remain vigilant, aware of their personal tendencies. They cultivate a strong work ethic and focus on achievement with a clear-eyed determination. In this manner, you can set healthy, significant life goals and be confident in achieving them, *if you are willing to do the work.* Then, no regrets.

YOUR CHOICES NOT ONLY CHANGE THE FORWARD
DIRECTION OF YOUR SHIP BUT CAN ALSO
ALTER ITS WAKE…

There is a way to change your past from this *moment onward.* To describe it in a linear manner, it does not alter what has come before this moment, but it does alter what comes after. When we set a new course, we pass through waters that we have not passed through before and would never have had the privilege of navigating if we hadn't set this particular course. Looking back, you can see that your course is now taking you into entirely different waters. It is a new way of thinking about the past, because in a general manner, you draw from your storehouse of memories (old courses) to determine what works and what does not.

Every thought matters. Every decision matters. When you understand that a choice you make now impacts your timeline in all directions, it offers you a fresh view of what has gone on before this moment, because you don't have to settle for the same old same old...from this moment on. You can change your life. It's a refreshing way of looking at the past.

A Constant Traveler Reminder:
LIFE-SPAN COUNTDOWN CALCULATION

It has been noted that the average life span of a person, from birth to death, is 30,000 days. The calculation below may come as a shock to you. Consider it an eye-opener. It can also be a game changer.

• Research the average life span for your gender in your country.*

• Convert that age into days by multiplying it by 365.25. This will give you the average life expectancy for your gender in terms of days.

• Take your age to the nearest month or one decimal place (for example, if you are 35 1/2 years old this month, use 35.5), and multiply that by 365.25. This will give you the actual number of days you have lived on this earth.

• Subtract this result from the previous result. This will give you, on the average, the number of days you have left to live before you begin defying the odds. *This does not mean you will die when the calculator reverts to 0,* but considering the

(continued)

---

odds, everything after can be considered bonus time!

Example: According to Statista.com, the average life span for a female living in Canada (as of 2017) is 84 years. If you are 35.5:

84 x 365.25 =   30,681

Current age (35.5) x 365.5 =   12,966.375 days lived

Days to average life expectancy: 17,714.625 days

If you are 50.5:

50.5 x 365.5 =   18,445.125 days lived

Days to average life expectancy: 12,235.875 days

Would I waste my money like I waste my time?

Consider how easy it is to spend $17,000 or $12,000. For many of us, that is the amount used on rent in one year or our five-year car loan or dining at a restaurant once a week for five short years. Being clear about the quality of your remaining time matters. Actuaries in the insurance industry use this type of information every day to calculate the statistical probability of future events.

Calculating the number of days the average Canadian female has on this earth was impactful for me. Seeing the average life expectancy for my son and husband (79 years, or 28,854.75 days) was a reality check. Even though it is a lot better than it was in 1920 (58.8), it still seems mighty short.

Working out my own calculations got me thinking about my purpose, the meaning of my life, and my contribution, as well as my personal legacy, and considering what I was going to do about it. The following are some questions I asked myself. I offer them to you for your consideration:

- Have I contributed to my family and my society?
- Have I been a positive or a negative contributor?
- What is my Give/Receive Balance?

*The statistical data available offers life-span information for males and females only. For those of you who gender-identify using a term other than male or female, use this as a guideline only. It is up to you to choose which most closely aligns to your current circumstances.

17

An Elegant Mind Demonstrates Its Freedom by Honoring the Freedom of Others.

It realizes that any attempt to control or manipulate another enslaves both parties.

Would you honor your own freedom if you did not honor my freedom to choose otherwise? Would you value your freedom of thought if you did not honor my freedom to think otherwise?

Otherwise—is there truly "other-wise," other *wisdom* of which you are not aware? Perhaps this awareness would revolutionize your own. Is that why you are afraid of it?

CAN FREEDOM BE OFFERED BY ITS CONSTRICTION?

Who is it that says you are wrong, you are lesser, you are unworthy, unless it is the part of you that acknowledges judgment's worth?

Do you expect those in your life to play by your sense of right? When you are focused on controlling what someone else is doing or saying, how does that focus restrict your ability to choose? When you are intent on changing the behavior of someone else (your child, spouse, sibling, friend, parent, co-worker), your world becomes smaller—is your attention and intention not directed toward something limited? In this situation, are your choices not dictated by another's actions?

ARE WE BOTH NOT HELD CAPTIVE WITHIN THESE WALLS?

When you expect someone else to relinquish their power to choose, you also give them your power to choose. This gift, grudgingly offered and resentfully accepted, fits neither of you. Inspiration offers other-wise. Through the inspired, there springs eternal other-wise, an infinite other-wise, offered from the wellspring of which we share and came to life to express.

You are nobody's savior, but you can be a collaborator. You do not grant permission, but you can offer freedom to others. You are not separate and alone, but you are connected to all things. Life is relationship.

It is not me, but we. *We* share this world with other living beings. Unless we acknowledge the interconnectedness of all things, we all may perish.

A Constant Traveler Reminder:
WRITE YOURSELF FREE

What is your definition of freedom? Write it out. The act of writing puts your thoughts in order.

Research the dictionary definition of *freedom*. How does it compare?

18

An Elegant Mind Sets Its Boundaries by Teaching Others How to Treat It.

You will allow others to abuse you to the extent that you feel you deserve it. You demonstrate your belief in how deserving you are of abuse by how much you willingly abuse yourself. It is beneficial to contemplate and clarify where you stand regarding self-abuse. Boundaries can be set in two fundamental ways:

1. Establishing clarity regarding your rights as a human being.

2. Creating your personal Standard of Excellence (SOE) and accepting no less from yourself or from others.

To establish boundaries, you must understand the unit of measurement: self-respect. Hold yourself in such high esteem as to clearly define your boundaries.

THOSE WHO REALIZE THEIR ELEGANCE SET THE
STANDARD FOR ITS APPRECIATION...

The Universal Declaration of Human Rights is the perfect place to begin. The following is shared from the website Youth for Human Rights: www.youthforhumanrights.org

United Nations Universal Declaration of Human Rights (Simplified Version)

1. We Are All Born Free and Equal. We are all born free. We all have our own thoughts and ideas. We should all be treated in the same way.

2. Don't Discriminate. These rights belong to everybody, whatever our differences.

3. The Right to Life. We all have the right to life, and to live in freedom and safety.

4. No Slavery. Nobody has any right to make us a slave. We cannot make anyone our slave.

5. No Torture. Nobody has any right to hurt us or to torture us.

6. You Have Rights No Matter Where You Go. I am a person just like you!

7. We're All Equal Before the Law. The law is the same for everyone. It must treat us all fairly.

8. Your Human Rights Are Protected by Law. We can all ask for the law to help us when we are not treated fairly.

9. No Unfair Detainment. Nobody has the right to put us in prison and keep us there, without good reason or to send us away from our country.

10. The Right to Trial. If we are put on trial, this should be in public. The people who try us should not let anyone tell them what to do.

11. We're Always Innocent till Proven Guilty. Nobody should be blamed for doing something until it is proven. When people say we did a bad thing, we have the right to show it is not true.

12. The Right to Privacy. Nobody Should Try to Harm Our Good Name. Nobody has the right to come into our home, open our letters, or bother us or our family without a good reason.

13. Freedom to Move. We all have the right to go where we want in our own country and to travel as we wish.

14. The Right to Seek a Safe Place to Live. If we are frightened of being badly treated in our own country, we all have the right to run away to another country to be safe.

15. Right to a Nationality. We all have the right to belong to a country.

16. Marriage and Family. Every adult has the right to marry and have a family if they want to. Men and women have the same rights when they are married, and when they are separated.

17. The Right to Your Own Things. Everyone has the right to own things or share them. Nobody should take our things from us without a good reason.

18. Freedom of Thought. We all have the right to believe in what we want to believe, to have a religion, or to change it if we want.

19. Freedom of Expression. We all have the right to make up our own minds, to think what we like, to say what we think, and to share our ideas with other people.

20. The Right to Public Assembly. We all have the right to meet our friends and to work together in peace to defend our rights. Nobody can make us join a group if we don't want to.

21. The Right to Democracy. We all have the right to take part in the government of our country. All adults should be allowed to choose their own leaders.

22. Social Security. We all have the right to affordable housing, medicine, education, and childcare, enough money to live on and medical help if we are ill or old.

23. Workers' Rights. Every adult has the right to do a job, to earn a fair wage for their work, and to join a trade union.

24. The Right to Play. We all have the right to rest from work and to relax.

25. Food and Shelter for All. We all have the right to a good life. Mothers and children, people who are old, unemployed or disabled, all people have the right to be cared for.

26. The Right to Education. Education is a right. Primary school should be free. We should learn about the United Nations and how to get on with others. We can choose what we learn.

27. Copyright. Copyright is a special law that protects one's own artistic creations and writings; others cannot make copies without permission. We all have the right to our own way of life and to enjoy the good things that art, science, and learning bring.

28. A Fair and Free World. There must be proper order, so we can all enjoy rights and freedoms in our own country and all over the world.

29. Responsibility. We have a duty to other people, and we should protect their rights and freedoms.

30. No One Can Take Away Your Human Rights.

STANDARD OF EXCELLENCE

A standard of excellence represents an uncompromising dedication to *your* best—not his, her, or their best.

EXCELLENCE VS. PERFECTION

Excellence is not perfection. Dedication to excellence is not about being perfect. It is about bringing your A game to the game every time. It is accepting nothing less than your very best in your interactions. Why?

• Because your time is valuable.

• Because your energy is valuable.

• Because you are worth your best effort.

• Because you have decided good enough isn't good enough.

• Because you are better than a substandard performance.

BUT I'M NOT THERE YET! I'M NOT EXCELLENT YET!

Excellence applies to students of all kinds—every student, not just high performers and accomplished, credentialed people. In fact, it applies especially to students because they are learning their craft, or the information in their class, or the skill set that will enable them to be successful in their chosen profession and, ultimately, in life. What you bring to the game matters.

PERFECTIONISM IS A FUNCTIONAL INABILITY TO DETERMINE VALUE...

When we believe everything is valuable, nothing is valuable. The perfectionist cannot parse the data to determine its essential value. Like a hoarder, they cannot let anything go.

This state, as a rule, has its roots in our personal values, beliefs, and assumptions about who we are. These formed early in life, when we began to differentiate as a person apart from our family of origin (parents or first caregivers). For whatever reason, we have accepted the idea that no matter what we do, we will never be enough—intelligent or good-looking or athletic or thin or strong or young or old enough to be worthy. We have trained our brains to idealize others. We set others up on pedestals that we believe are perpetually out of our reach. To be accepted as worthy, we believe that we must think, say, and do everything to perfection. In the world of the perfectionist, it is all or nothing. Galvanized by perfectionism, most perfectionists would rather do nothing than be less than ideal. With the diversity of almost 8 billion people living on this planet, how can this possibly be an appropriate response?

CAN EVERY PERSON ADHERE TO YOUR STANDARD OF PERFECTION?

Perfectionism is true only in relation to you. Yes, the truth is that there will always be someone who exhibits greater traits or has better features than you. If you are now at the top of your game, given the time and circumstance, it is certain to change as you age and new players are introduced. *So being enough must be about something other than what we cannot do or be.*

ARE YOU AFRAID TO FAIL?

Failure begins and ends with our thoughts about it. Until you accept it, *f-a-i-l* is just another four-letter F-word. Let's creatively reframe the F-word by deleting the word *fail* from our vocabulary and substituting it for some new F-words: *fearless faith, focus, and fortitude* (see Statement 2 for review).

When you label me, you negate me. —Soren Kierkegaard

I take this statement to mean that who you think I am says more about who I am not than about who I am. However, I believe Kierkegaard gives too much credit to external forces. Where is my personal power in this scenario? After much thought, I have begun to consider this quote from another perspective:

WHEN I LABEL ME, I CREATE ME...

When I accept a l-a-b-e-l, that is when it becomes a *label*. Until then, it is just five letters strung together. Acceptance is key. Furthermore, when I choose to adopt a label (a pronouncement of who *I am*), I, in effect, create me:

I am a man, a woman, androgynous, transsexual, genderless, etc.

I am a Muslim, Christian, Buddhist, Taoist, atheist, agnostic, etc.

I am outspoken, athletic, stubborn, ugly, optimistic, depressed, proactive, extroverted...a loser...old...

Who are you without your label? Your personal tag that says "Do Not Remove Under Penalty of Law"? Before you accept a label, it is always wise to consider if you are going to like, let alone love, your creation.

Excellence is elegant. Perfectionism is pernicious...

DEVELOPING YOUR STANDARD OF EXCELLENCE

A Standard of Excellence falls within three separate domains:

1. The Thoughtful domain

2. The Expressive domain

3. The Active domain

The following are some suggestions for you to begin to develop your personal Standard of Excellence in each of the three domains. I have provided some category suggestions as a starting point. Keep in mind that you will be creating *guidelines* for excellence in all aspects of life—you will not always be able to live this way.

Perfectionism recognizes ideals; excellence recognizes mastery.

THE THOUGHTFUL DOMAIN

Motto: Thought is a selection process.

Example: Ask yourself the question, How do I express excellence in my *greetings and farewells*? What are your thoughts as you interact with others? Set your intention as to how you wish each relationship in your life to progress—the energy and attitude with which you engage others.
• I will meet my partner with a smile.
• I will ensure he understands that I care about his presence in my life and his contribution to this day.
• I will let her know I love her.
• I will listen to him.
• I will take each farewell as if it may be the last time I see her.

How do I express excellence in…?
• Self-care
• Compassion
• Gentleness
• Happiness
• Peace
• Mindful awareness

- The elegant arts—appreciation, patience, forgiveness, acceptance, freedom, silence, and trust

THE EXPRESSIVE DOMAIN

Motto: Think twice, speak once.

Example: Ask yourself the question, How do I express excellence through *entertainment*—does what I watch and listen to fill my mind with nourishment and inspiration?
- I will choose to watch movies, television, and videos and to listen to podcasts that inspire, uplift, energize, and teach me something new each day.
- I will offer this beneficial information to others.
- I will recommend these beneficial movies, programs, or sites to others.

How do I express excellence in...?
- Conversation
- Writing
- Online
- Reading
- Music or other audio

THE ACTIVE DOMAIN

Motto: Govern yourself accordingly.

Example: Ask yourself the question, How do I express excellence in *performance*—what energy and effort do I bring to my day (my work, my play)?

- I will give 100% because my life, my work, and my playtime are worth the effort.
- When I agree to do something with someone (or for someone), I will show up on time, and they will get nothing less than my best.
- I will embody a person who I would be proud to call my friend.
- I will perform with an energy that does not intentionally cause trouble or difficulty for others.

How do I express excellence in…?
- Relationships (family of origin, intimate, friendships, community, workplace)
- Personal conduct
- Productivity
- Activity

A Constant Traveler Reminder:
YOUR PERSONAL STANDARD OF EXCELLENCE

Develop your own Standard of Excellence using the outline above. Execute it.

19

An Elegant Mind Expresses Honesty with Regard to Its Endeavors and Accomplishments.

It does not view them as a source of pride that sets itself apart from others. Conversely, it does not undermine them but simply states what is.

ACCOMPLISHMENTS ARE WHAT THEY ARE—
STEPS ON A LADDER...

Imagine that you have been provided with a well-designed, sturdy ladder made from common everyday materials. This tool, as ladders do, is guaranteed to take you to a destination. Would you brag about your ladder or its steps? Would you value some steps more than others?

Could you acknowledge that your son, your daughter, your friend, your co-worker, your competitor, your ex-spouse—or someone you view as your enemy—also has a ladder very much like yours? And even though you notice that they are not as far up their ladder as you are, which is more practical: watching them, or watching where you are placing your own feet and your own hands?

What if they have a newer ladder or have reached a step or two higher than you have? What if they have reached the very top? Are you inspired or defeated by their accomplishment? Would you try to knock them off?

We are not and cannot be devoid of ego. That is the confusion. The ego is not our enemy; we created it to keep us alive. We need our ego to negotiate life, but when we *identify* as our ego, we have become unbalanced. There is more to life than survival. We must engage our creativity and inspiration, thereby disengaging the "survival of the fittest" perspective of the ego in order to thrive.

The key is to live with courage and conviction, to have our ego serve us, and to not allow it to serve itself.

Overstating accomplishments is aggrandizement.
Overinflating accomplishments is deception.
Undermining accomplishment—ours or others'—is tragedy...

A Constant Traveler Reminder:
BE SOMEONE'S INSPIRATION

Who can you encourage, appreciate, coach, mentor, or guide today?

20

An Elegant Mind Does Not Compete with Others or Desire What Others Have.

It knows there is always room for one more.

Desire your success; do not desire the success of others. Your success is not contingent on the failure of others.

If you assume there will never be enough, you will always be right. So, what if you choose to operate on the assumption that there is *way more than enough*?

Thinking that you are less will not bring you more. Hasn't your past proven that it brings you less?

THE PLEASURE ADDICTION

Winning creates a pleasure response through the release of endorphins that losing does not. Endorphins are our intrinsic reward system, but when they become habitual—a craving— they can be addictive. We want more, and when we don't get more, we begin to resent those who seem to have more of what we want. On some level we fear meeting our competitors because we know that they have the power to take away our pleasure. Sometimes this fear is enough to make us give up before we even begin.

Does your competition represent the loss of your pleasure? Is your fierce response to engage in competition because you are fighting to feel pleasure, something you obviously lack or find in short supply?

There was a commercial on television a couple of years ago that presented as a humorous situation a guy who was celebrating because he worked all his life to be second-best. We laughed and agreed that the guy was pathetic.

DID YOU EVER QUESTION THE FACT THAT SECOND-BEST IS STILL REALLY DARN GOOD?

Have you ever used the statement "Always the bridesmaid, never the bride"? Remembered the words spoken by Sean Connery in the movie *Highlander*, "In the end there can be only one"? Who sets this damn bar? We do! We seduce ourselves and others with our fantasies of what happiness is, what winning is, and what satisfaction means. Isn't it time we look at how we define success?

It is statistically impossible to win all the time. It is statistically improbable to win the majority of the time—unless, that is, you *reframe* what winning means to you. Success can equal winning in one manner (when we practice what Stephen Covey terms as *win-win* in his business classic *The 7 Habits of Highly Effective People*) when we understand that true success lies in this elegant mind-set—when what truly benefits one benefits all in some manner, everyone wins.

A Constant Traveler Reminder:
EXAMINE YOUR COMPETITIVE STYLE

Consider what competition means—a contest or game. It can also mean conflict (as in fighting, rivalry, vying), or it can refer to a competitor (as in the foe, the enemy, the opposition). Informally it means "keeping up with the Joneses."

Is it important to you to compete? Why or why not?

Anxiety is the handmaiden of contemporary ambition.
—Alain de Botton

21

An Elegant Mind Endorses That Which Is Truly Helpful.

It does not dwell on mistakes—
its own or those of others.

You are inherently worthy. Give yourself
permission to ask for what you need. Don't
bludgeon your dreams with doubt...

Error does not have to indicate failure; it highlights the
necessity for a course correction. By dwelling on mistakes,
it changes an opportunity for learning into a reason for suffering. Dwelling on errors does not encourage anyone. Instead,
it serves to denigrate both parties. The point of this is that the
person who dwells on errors disrespects themselves and others
as well. Consider a mistake a *mis-take*—as in a take that did not
quite make the cut—a goof, a blooper.

Everywhere you go, you take one person with you—you.
How comfortable are you with your personal traveling companion, your Constant Traveler? Being comfortable alone
means you will be more joyful in a relationship, as you will have
learned to fill your own needs to an elegant degree, and what

you bring to your relationships will benefit all concerned. It will be mutual give-and-take.

Failure is learned behavior. —Bishop T.D. Jakes

If failure is learned behavior, then unlearn it. That is success. Face your fears one by one. Learn to be assertive one step at a time. Be comfortable hearing your own voice, and give yourself permission (over and over if need be—make it your motto) to feel your own power. Recognize no man or woman as your personal guru.

If you do not make these adjustments, you will unconsciously attract and be attracted to another person with the same confused vibe that you are emitting.

WILL YOUR VIBE DETERMINE YOUR TRIBE, OR WILL YOU LET YOUR TRIBE DETERMINE YOUR VIBE?

Learn from your past bloopers. Let them make you stronger.

A Constant Traveler Reminder:
FACE YOUR FEAR

Consider your most easily attainable life goal. What fears are blocking you from beginning to accomplish this goal?
- Fear of public speaking
- Fear of embarrassment or ridicule
- Fear of losing money
- Fear of not being accepted
- Fear of trying and failing
- Fear of others' judgment
- Fear of not fitting in
- Other fears:

_____

_____

_____

Education is illumination! What small step can you take right now that will help you begin to build confidence and overcome this fear?
- Read a book or articles on the subject
- Journal about it—write it out
- Talk to a supportive family member, friend, coach, or counselor
- Take a course
- Join a club or group
- Other ideas:

_____

_____

_____

Success is failure unlearned!

22

An Elegant Mind Governs Its Thoughts and Words with Wisdom.

Y ou select your thoughts just as carefully as your words. You select the words you speak just as carefully as you select the words you write. An elegant mind imagines your thoughts as if they are written in stone. It asks, "Are you ready for these to survive you?"

WHAT DID YOU SAY?

Listening is an art. Comprehension involves release—an open mind, a loving mind, a quiet mind.

Ever play a party game called Telephone? The players form a line, and the first player whispers a message into the ear of the second person in line. That person whispers the message to the next person in line, and so on, until the message reaches the person at the end of the line. That person then announces the message to the entire group. Even though each person tries to relate the message as they heard it, the result at the end is often a very different message from what was originally whispered.

When we consider how thought gets transformed into words and words get transformed into action, we realize the distinct probability that we will be misunderstood. It is not a possibility; it is a probability. When you verbalize a thought, there is already a disconnect as you search for words. You may not realize that this is what you are doing, because there are many words you have memorized and use as your "go-to" language. However, the world is full of synonyms that seem the same but are completely different.

EVERYTHING I SAY MAY BE LIES. IT IS TRUE TO ME,
BUT YOU CAN PROVE IT UNTRUE...

Your perspective is demonstrated by your linguistic bias and limited by your knowledge of the subject of which you are expressing. Have you ever said something and then stated it another way? *In other words,* expressed yourself and then attempted to clarify your statement with other words? The words you choose are few of many possible and there is a high probability that you will be misunderstood, especially if you think you know about that which you are speaking.

Thinking is not enough. To know is to road-test the hypothesis through living. *To express knowing through living is wisdom.* You prove your hypotheses every moment of your life, but that only serves to make them true to you.

We say that *Love is all there is* while we are crying into our beer that we don't know or have love. *How can this be true?*

You lament, "I never get what I want!"

Life says, "What do you want?"

You say, "I don't know!"

Didn't you just receive it?

Today's Declaration: My word is LAW. —T. Harv Eker

A Constant Traveler Reminder:

EXAMINE YOUR
PERSONAL VERNACULAR

Do you use curse words a lot? How does that serve you?
What saying do you use a lot? Ask a friend or family
member if you cannot think of one that you use often.
How does it serve you?

May you taste your words before you spit them out.
—Irish proverb

23

An Elegant Mind Does Not Accept Detours, Because It Is Always Arriving.

It does not attempt to make the road shorter
but travels it in such a manner that every
action leaves the land more fertile and the
landscape more beautiful.

WHEN WILL I KNOW THAT I HAVE ARRIVED?

Have you ever noticed how much you focus on the future, always wishing away today? As in, *I can hardly wait for spring to get here.... When I grow up, nobody will tell me what to do.... When I am successful, I will have the life of my dreams...* You cannot seem to find a way to fill your need for more. What will happen if you never feel you have what you need?

Consider how you plod along at your job, always working for the weekend while dreaming of the day when you can be on permanent vacation. How many of you truly despise today? Do you prefer to substitute it for daydreams and fantasies?

We tend to make ourselves victims of the "shoulda, coulda, wouldas": *I shoulda zigged instead of zagged. I coulda done that, but now it's too late. I woulda done that if only things had been different.*

This resistance manifests as a restlessness, a vague just-can't-quite-put-my-finger-on-it dissatisfaction with what is happening right now. It keeps you constantly trolling for something—internet, books, music, activity, the next relationship—to hook your attention, to provide distraction. White noise. Constant chatter. Competition. Contention. Condescension. Exercising your Superiority Quotient. These are some of the detours to which I refer. *They are not worthy of your attention.*

If you are one of those elegant people living an artful life, then you do not look for ways to crash the line, because you understand that where you are right now is exactly where you are supposed to be given your understanding of life and of the world. You survey the terrain with clear eyes from this perspective in order to appreciate how far you have come. You offer gratitude for everything, no matter how mundane, because you see the land and the landscape as sacred and understand that you may never pass this way again. You realize it is the only way in which to truly live.

THIS DOES NOT MEAN YOU MUST GIVE UP YOUR
DESIRE TO BE ALL THAT YOU CAN BE.

You are worthy of the big picture you see in your mind. The guiding force of the big picture is much larger than any objective or achievement. It means you are mindful of *what you are creating now, because it will be what is returned to you as your future. As in, The Law of the Harvest.*

IF LOVE IS THE PLANT, THEN GRATITUDE IS ITS BUD.
IF GRATITUDE IS THE BUD, THEN JOY IS ITS FLOWER.
IT IS MY DESIRE THAT MY DAYS ARE ALWAYS
INFUSED WITH ITS FRAGRANCE...

A Constant Traveler Reminder:
WAY MORE THAN ENOUGH

What if there is nowhere to go and nothing to become?
What if you are way more than enough exactly as you are?
I love myself today has become my personal motto.
Use this statement as a prompting to find the words that
define your personal appreciation of life.

Just take a little walk with me
Let's talk about your destiny.
I'll show you, you're a diamond in the rough.
Step out and feel the wind once more…
Time to spread your wings and soar
above it all…
'Cause if you could see what I can see,
You're way more than enough.
Way more than enough.

—From the song "Way More" by PDT

24

An Elegant Mind Knows That What It Expects, It Asks for and Receives.

It acknowledges and understands the value of,
"I give, I receive, I see what I believe."

I look about and see what I believe
And thusly so,
I give what I receive.
This Eden past, no comfort there for me
I can but weep...
'Tis pleasure's barren bones that pierce my feet.
My god, who is it I perceive?
Which versions since revised, revered, and bastardized
shall I decide to keep?
In sight, I seek
A glimpse of peace
and I, untethered,
free'd to dance with naked joy
will surely take my leave.

—PDT

Right this moment, would you give over total control of your entire life to a nine-year-old child? Even if that was your nine-year-old self? Research in human development has discovered that the beliefs, values, and assumptions with which we negotiate the adult world are set firmly in place by the time we are nine years old. The nine-year-old has searched and found answers to such questions as: Who truly understands me? Who loves me? Who cares what I think? Can I ask for what I need? What are my talents? My strengths and weaknesses? Am I smart? Capable? Athletic? Creative?

But the most important question that gets answered by your nine-year-old mind is, *Am I enough just the way I am?*

Every choice we make, every decision and move from then on is weighed by these beliefs and values about how the world is, not by how the world should be or could be or would be.

HOW THE WORLD IS...

These beliefs have formed the basis for our adult lives. Our subsequent experiences create the assumption that we can expect more of the same. This is what is meant by a self-fulfilling prophesy. If we haven't explored these in an adult manner that allows us to determine if they are what we *truly believe* or if they were handed to us by our parents, our family, and our society, can we *truly say they are ours*? How do we know if they serve us at this stage in our lives? What if some of the conclusions we made when we were nine years old are still running the show? What if there is a more inspired way to negotiate the world?

Now is the perfect time to take
responsibility for your life.

I give, I receive, and I see what I believe. This is a statement of the circular nature of give-and-take. Your thought stream includes those thoughts that are self-nurturing as well those that are self-defeating. Your life situation at this moment shows you on which side of balance you are currently navigating.

A Constant Traveler Reminder:
EXPRESS YOURSELF!

Research has shown that if you take the time to exercise your thoughts in writing, you have a 40% chance of accomplishing your goal. It has also revealed that if you share them, you have an 80% chance of completing this goal! Expressing your thoughts in writing will allow you to explore and clarify your values and beliefs. It may help to discuss your results with a trusted friend, family member, mentor, or coach.

VALUES

Take some time to determine what you truly value. If you search on the internet, you will find many lists that will spark your creativity. List as many as apply.

You will find that many of these values are similar. Group these values into categories.

Summarize your list to the three that hold the most value. *You may discover that these are also your three prime motivators in life.*

Why are these so important for you?

(continued)

Consider your earliest memory of when each of these values was formed:

- What person do you most associate with this value?
- Where did you first apply it?
- How did you first apply it?
- Has your outlook on this value changed over time?

Example: Perhaps one of your core values is connection. Thinking back to your childhood, you can see where this was formed:

1. Social connection was something your family deeply valued and celebrated. This value was reinforced through your culture and community. It is priceless to you. You have made it yours, and it has become part of your personal and professional way of living.

2. You did not feel connected to someone in your family in a way that satisfied this need. Perhaps you view yourself as an outcast in some manner. Your need for connection remains an unfulfilled ache in you, a wounded spot that continues to haunt you in adult life. You feel lonely a lot of the time.

This is the time to remember that you are no longer a child. You have the ability and resources available to you to make your need for connection work for you. As an adult, you can take action and find deeper and richer connections with others in a way that satisfies this need. It will take courage. You must act, and this may mean asking for help, but it can be done.

A TATTOO MOMENT...

These explorations create what I consider a *tattoo moment*—a memory that has become tattooed on your mind and serves as a permanent reminder of where you've been and how far you've come since then.

ROCK YOUR WISE!

Apply gratitude to the memory—either that you had the experience or that you survived it.

Keep in mind that everyone has a story, and we all can benefit from the support and encouragement of others. You are not alone. Celebrate how far you've come since then! Used in this way, *a tattoo moment* can help you to live your best, most elegant life.

BELIEFS

Take some time to examine your personal beliefs about how the world is. Beliefs have generally been considered in the same context as values, but you may find that the two are not necessarily the same.

Beliefs are formed from many areas of life:

- Religious/spiritual beliefs that we have been taught
- Beliefs about our family culture and the culture and rules of our society
- Beliefs about who we are and our value as a person
- Beliefs about the world we live in as a result our personal experiences

(continued)

Write a list of your personal beliefs. Consider your earliest memory of when each of these beliefs was formed:

• What person do you most associate with this belief?
• Where did you first apply it?
• How did you first apply it?
• Has your outlook on this belief changed over time?

Do your conclusions represent who you are now?

Consider whether this statement is true for you: *You live the best you can each day from what you know for sure. When you know better, you do better.*

Do you believe that if you receive new insight, your values and beliefs can change? Why or why not?

25

An Elegant Mind Practices Letting Go.

It does not struggle with sticky fingers, where the
past still clings to them because it won't let go.

ALONE TOGETHER

Lo, I was lost, but now I see
that what's for others, not for me.
This bloodless land not meant to be
my home, or yours, so why don't we
continue on this path unknown,
for surely this
is not our home.
On and on and on we roam,
on farther down this lonely road
our blistr'd feet, this heavy load
we whisper,
"Leave this truth untold…"
And don't look up, there is no sun!
Just follow me, as I've begun
to realize this barren path on which

all others too must pass,

is desperate long,

our journey fast.

This final thrust, their truth undone

for all their speak of light and sun that heals…

Indeed, they are the foolish ones.

Who'll nurse their wounds when evil's won?

So, steady on,

my chosen one.

Yes, they cry love but cannot see

these darkest dreams of you and me.

You are like me and not like she.

On this sharp point

we well agree.

And oh, the silly games they play,

content to pay another day!

They say there is another way, but

they don't know what we've been through,

what we've endured,

just me and you.

Our wretched task it tracks us still,

and we alone must gather will.

Our fingers ache, to let it go.

Plead as we will,

it lingers so…

We know and know and know the cause!

Those babes, they just can't see Its claws.

So love them well until they die,

and shield them well as past goes by,

but batten'd down for stormy weather

we soldier on.

Alone together.

Our dark-cast sisters know the mire,
who taste its blood, charred in its fire,
and breathe its ash 'til we expire.
We broken ones, we claim our right
to cling to it with all our might.
This heaving cloak well-soaked with sweat,
relentlessly, with bated breath,
it hounds our heels,
lest we forget.

—PDT

Our Ancestral Legacy of Dysfunction

Healing our family's legacy of dysfunction is acceptance of it, owning our part in it, and making a conscious decision to act with compassion. It begins with a declaration of "No more! This legacy stops here! My inheritance will no longer be my children's burden." This means taking stock of what was dumped on you as a child raised in a dysfunctional environment and handing it back to your ancestors. You cauterize the ancient energetic bleed that has overwhelmed your own spirit.

This is not an easy feat, especially if your parent(s) are still living. The energetic conduit that has been functioning since childhood remains intact (sometimes on a subtle level, as you have learned to live with it). It is vital to begin the task of freeing yourself from this influence. Applying the gifts of compassion reignites your vitality.

If your parent(s) have died, the process is different. The energetic bleed has been severed abruptly, and there will be a period (months or years) when you experience disorientation. This is a huge change. Change is role adjustment. *Who are you without your parent? How do you view a world without your parent in it?* Loss of love, loyalty, attachment, nostalgia, guilt, and regret mix together to make this task of freeing yourself different from those whose parent still lives. The difference is that with death, the conduit that has been motivating you is closed. The common elements noted above, however, are every bit as draining and difficult.

For those of you who are parents, it is time to own your personal "caca." This ownership begins with an honest appraisal of what it is that you have dumped on your offspring in the name of love and, verbally and energetically, take it back.

This caca looks like expectations. Do I expect my children to...?

- Always be there for me
- Respect me no matter what I do or say
- Listen to me before I listen to them
- Believe like me
- Forgive my failings without understanding
- Live the conditions of my dreams for them
- Make me and my family proud
- Accept my advice
- Shield me from loneliness
- Take care of me, emotionally or physically
- Pay my way
- Deny their own pain because I can't stand it
- Sacrifice themselves to save me
- Accept our family's painful legacy each time I feel like regurgitating it
- Express gratitude for my efforts

This, my friend, is what toxic waste looks like in real life. Releasing your children from the *chains of your expectations* and letting them know that they are accepted simply for who they are—simply by being your kid—frees you both.

Walking this talk in daily life is a perpetual act of love. You can do this today. Acting with compassion and intention, from where you sit now, stems the flow both ways. It is always the perfect time to begin.

A Constant Traveler Reminder:
LEAVING HOME

Can you ever go home again? This age-old question leads us to deeper insights when we consider that *we may never have truly left.*

Who will you be when you set yourself free of the role you have played all your life?

Consider where you can benefit from ancestral healing today and, with elegance, begin to either take back whatever toxicity you may have inadvertently dumped on others or give back the toxicity that you may have inadvertently taken on.

26

An Elegant Mind Does Not Indulge in Self-importance.

Cambridge.org defines *indulge* as: 1. To allow yourself or another person to have something enjoyable, especially more than is good for you; 2. To give someone anything they want and not mind if they behave badly.

HOW CAN I GET OVER MY FINE SELF?

Superiority is failure—failure to connect, to listen, to observe, to accept the gifts of others, to be creative, to be inclusive, to thrive, and to live well. Life is relationship. Superiority is separation.

When you are elite, you reject others based on your personal criteria—when you are so right that you reject another's version of right as valid, when you act as if your map is the only map to a destination you all share. You believe that your value is superior and that their value is inferior. You overvalue your own contribution and undervalue the contribution of others.

Superiority is an indicator of a poor leader, one that is doomed to fail because they can't fall.

Superiority is insidious. Elitist, separatist thoughts slowly become part of your language and part of your life. Your tone and the spirit with which it is delivered change as you condescend. What you choose to see hypnotizes you and reinforces your vision of yourself as vitally important.

YOU ARE ONLY AS SUCCESSFUL AS YOUR INTEGRITY.
YOUR INTEGRITY DETERMINES YOUR SUCCESS...

Merriam-Webster's defines self-importance as an exaggerated sense of one's own value or importance. Synonyms include *arrogance, conceit,* and *pomposity.* There are two dark aspects of self-importance. One is an inflated sense of one's own importance, and the other is an inflated sense of one's own unimportance.

Indulgence in self-importance involves the callous disregard for others' feelings. It is conditional self-regard—the opposite of *unconditional positive regard,* the foundation of self-worth, confidence, and therapeutic practice.

SELF-APPRECIATION MORPHS INTO SELF-IMPORTANCE
THROUGH SELF-INDULGENCE...

How often do you pass judgment and label a person a narcissist? A clinical diagnosis of narcissistic behavior disorder must be determined by a licensed professional and meet specific criteria. Generally, the true narcissist is a survivor of a traumatic childhood. Narcissism is a maladaptation that an individual makes to survive.

Many times, you take on the role of an armchair clinician and conclude that a self-centered person who has the *audacity* to ignore *you* or tick *you* off is a narcissist. Whether this is true or not doesn't matter if you believe it. What matters is that you feel good about yourself. It's true, that label certainly looks better on them than it would on you.

Granted, there are times when a self-centered person breaches your boundaries and causes misery that can impact you for a lifetime. This is totally and understandably tragic, especially if you have the misfortune of being reared by someone like this. It may be beneficial to consider that, under different circumstances, that person could be you or me.

ARE YOU SELFIE-IMPORTANT?

If a researcher were to "creep" your social media or analyze your computer's history, what conclusions would they draw? What would they determine as your pattern of behavior, your personal style, your way of looking at the world? Your beliefs?

Let's consider that the conclusions these researchers arrive at matter to you monetarily. Will they be used to make or break that interview for the job you really, really want? Influence your personal success? Solidify friendships? Or raise your vibe as well as the vibe of your tribe?

WELL, THEY MAY, AND THEY MIGHT, AND THEY DO.

How do you think you would fare? Would the researchers conclude that you are happy or unhappy? Pessimistic or optimistic? Self-depreciating, self-promoting...*selfie-important*?

Does your content reveal you to be content, discontent, or malcontent? It may be an interesting exercise to ask a person you feel will be truthful with you to check it out and offer you feedback.

If you don't use social media for personal reasons or don't use social media at all, how do you consider those who do?

Social media acts like a two-way mirror. It reflects your innermost thoughts to the world while simultaneously revealing your inner sanctum.

A Constant Traveler Reminder:
MINDFUL SCROLLING

While you are scrolling through posts today, be mindful of what hooks your attention. Be mindful of where you feel the urge to comment, and why.

27

An Elegant Mind Holds No Other Accountable for Its Experiences.

INVICTUS

The poem that inspired Nelson Mandela while in prison.

Out of the night that covers me,
Black as the pit from pole to pole,
I thank whatever gods may be
For my unconquerable soul.

In the fell clutch of circumstance
I have not winced nor cried aloud.
Under the bludgeonings of chance
My head is bloody, but unbowed.

Beyond this place of wrath and tears
Looms but the Horror of the shade,
And yet the menace of the years
Finds and shall find me unafraid.

It matters not how strait the gate,
How charged with punishments the scroll,
I am the master of my fate,
I am the captain of my soul.

by William Ernest Henley

L ife is like a sailing ship, and you are the captain. You may be part of a vast multi-ship flotilla, but you are at your ship's helm. Even if you didn't seem to ask for a command, you have it. You may choose to sail a well-traveled route, or you may be inspired by new, open waters. As you sail along, there is generally plenty of fair weather. If you are wise, that is where you learn as much as you can about skillful navigation. You know there will be storms and lulls in this journey, because you have observed others as they weather theirs, and perhaps you have weathered some storms and lulls yourself.

IT'S ALL SACRED SPACE OR NOTHING IS SACRED SPACE…

Regardless, you cannot give the helm of this boat to another sailor, no matter how close to you he or she is sailing. You decide whether to open your sails and catch the full gale. This could mean joyously speeding toward an exciting objective, or it could mean a reckless endangerment of your ship. You decide whether to trim the sails back and navigate the course with a steady, sure hand. This could mean working toward your objective at a slower pace because you are introspective and wise, or this could mean you are deathly afraid of a wreck and want to follow closely in someone else's wake. At different points in your life, opening the sails or trimming them back could represent living in balance.

You decide. If you don't, no worries. You will float along. The ocean does its thing regardless. Whether you follow someone else's course or follow your own inner directives, navigating this water is new to you. Each decision is an adjustment in course correction that opens the door to a whole new world. It is how now works. Each increment of time represents the manifestation of those thoughts on which you focus. Each moment is now. How you choose to experience it is your choice. You choose where you stand. Or float.

Do you stand at the stern, ruefully observing your wake and resisting your course? Do you stand at the bow, impulsively professing to be the "monarch of the world," at the mercy of whatever blows through? Most of us do not regard our moment-to-moment decisions in this manner. We go about our lives, waffling between being reluctantly dragged through the moments and angrily letting randomness carry us along.

Consider the effectiveness of a sailor who, realizing that they truly despise the course on which they find themselves, gives up the helm and decides to blow as hard as he or she can into the sails. How do you think the wind and the ocean will respond?

There is a third option, one that represents skillful, balanced navigation. If this person does not like the direction in which they are sailing, the wise captain surveys the situation and utilizes the experience and wisdom of those traveling with them. The captain also understands that he or she has the collective wisdom of the ages at their fingertips.

A WISE CAPTAIN UNDERSTANDS THAT OTHERS ARE THE TRUE NAVIGATION POINTS OF THIS JOURNEY.

There is value in sharing your personal experiences as well as welcoming the experiences of others. Consult with others, those who have charted this course and are willing to share their map with you. They may demonstrate their reasoning as well as their technique and show you what instruments they have used, but you must learn how to use those instruments, and you must apply those techniques. You understand that their mapping skills were learned by trial and error, just the way you are learning yours. Their coordinates may or may not be totally accurate. In fact, most times the one who offers their course to you captains a ship with evidence of having weathered many storms themselves. Someone else in the flotilla may offer you a totally different map.

It is up to you to summon the courage to commit to one course or another—to zig or zag—and accept responsibility for your decision.

It is always the best course of action to understand the specifications of your own ship, how it handles in every kind of weather.

It is beneficial to observe the waters in which you alone sail, with courage.

It is wise to consider the course with an open mind, eager to discover and utilize new navigational instruments.

It is inspiring and confidence building to any captain at any age to navigate these waters with others. Offer them gratitude, because without them, you founder even in the calmest of seas.

A Constant Traveler Reminder:
SEVEN AREAS OF INFLUENCE

This questionnaire is designed to assist you in determining the **top two areas of life** that you feel would benefit from personal development. In the box provided, write the number that most accurately correlates with your agreement with the following statements. Consider higher numbers to be a spotlight being shined on areas that require your attention.

1: Very much like me

2: Mostly like me

3: Somewhat like me

4: Not much like me

5: Not like me at all

1. Family:

I enjoy a rewarding relationship with (choose ONE of the following):

☐ My spouse or significant other

☐ I prefer to remain single

I enjoy a healthy relationship with (choose ONE of the following):

☐ My child/children

☐ I have chosen not to have children

☐ I enjoy close relationships with my family (parents, siblings, other family and/ or in-laws)

☐ I have friends who feel like family to me

☐ I regularly celebrate significant milestones with family

Score _____ (continued)

2. Social:

☐ I enjoy close and rewarding friendships
☐ I am part of a group that serves others
☐ I volunteer time and/or funds on a regular basis
☐ I enjoy leisure activities with others
☐ I regularly engage in community events

Score _____

3. Personal Development:

☐ I have created a personal development plan
☐ I have created a personal Standard of Excellence*
☐ I actively pursue my hobbies and leisure interests on a regular basis
☐ I am dedicated to continuous learning and personal improvement
☐ I have clear and attainable life goals and am working toward them

Score _____

4. Financial:

☐ I am a good money manager
☐ I have a secure financial plan—short term
☐ I pay myself first
☐ I have an emergency fund
☐ I have a secure financial plan—long term

Score _____

5. Career:

☐ I am actively engaged in professional growth (reading, learning)

☐ I am clear about what I value about my work

☐ I am committed to excellence in all that I do

☐ I know where I am going with my career

☐ I have established a network of supportive colleagues

Score _____

6. Physical:

☐ I exercise two to three times a week for a minimum of 30 minutes each time

☐ I do resistance training (strength training)

☐ I do aerobic conditioning (walking, running, biking, swimming, skiing)

☐ I do daily flexibility exercises (stretching, yoga)

☐ I plan my meals, eat at regular times, and choose nutritious food

Score _____

7. Spiritual:

☐ I feel inspired and motivated most days

☐ I feel a connection with something greater than myself

☐ My life has meaning

☐ I live a purposeful life

☐ I practice mindfulness and meditation regularly

Score _____   (continued)

List the two areas with the highest score:

Primary area: _____

Score _____

Secondary area: _____

Score _____

Consider this a general overview of the seven areas that influence your life. The areas with the highest score are *suggested* starting points—you choose your priority.

* See Your Personal Standard of Excellence
(on page 96)

28

An Elegant Mind Honors Its Teachers as the Source of Its Resourcefulness.

An aspect of elegance is dedication to continual learning. The elegant mind is the beginner's mind. It is the open, receptive mind of the student.

There is always something to be learned from any experience if you choose for it to be so. In this circumstance, you focus on the positive aspects of experience because focusing on the negative doesn't serve your best life. The emphasis here is that you don't allow any person or situation to bring you down.

Teachers come in all forms. Some are pleasant; many are not. The wise student discovers the value in each style of teaching. The student may not have asked for this curriculum but appreciates it for what can be gained from it.

APPRECIATION IS AN INDICATOR OF THE STUDENT'S
MASTERY OF THE MATERIAL...

A Constant Traveler Reminder:
GATHERING RESOURCES

Consider each experience from a position of resourcefulness:

1. What *positive thing* can you take away from this situation?

2. What *skills* did this person or situation help you develop, even if it was by modeling its opposite?

3. What has this experience brought you in terms of *empathy and compassion* for others who have had similar experiences?

4. How has your behavior *changed for the better* by having known this person or having lived through this experience?

5. How have you *grown* by knowing them? What would you describe as your triumphant post-traumatic growth experience that may also benefit others?

29

An Elegant Mind Realizes That Perception Is Highly Subjective.

It maintains a high level of transparency
and authenticity. It offers a loving perspective
by allowing another mind to share—or to
not share—its version of truth.

PERCY AND EVE

This is the story of Percy.

This is the story of Eve.

Eve descended directly as outlined in *The Script*. Percy still says he never descended at all.

They met one warm spring day in June. The birds were singing. The flowers were blooming. Love was in the air. It was love at first sight, just like in the storybooks.

Percy felt himself like he had never felt himself before. He grew as she smiled. In her brown eyes, he was a champion!

Eve understood pain. She found herself in it. She was its savior. Giving was her shield, her temperance, and her example. She gave herself away to it.

When she met Percy, she began to see rightly. Clearly. She

felt the vague stirrings of her own power, long clearly denied. Her mother's mother knew what she was thinking.

Percy and Eve created a child.

"Let's teach our child to walk and talk and how to save us," they said, at least to themselves. And so, they did.

They don't remember the exact moment when each turned to the other with suspicious eyes, but by its effects, they both assumed it happened while the other wasn't looking. That changed the water on the beans.

Percy feared *The Script* more than he feared Eve, and that was a lot. After all this time, she had taken his power. She must have stolen it, again, while he wasn't looking.

"How could I have been so blind?" became his mantra.

Eve made good on her word. She gave and gave without receiving. She knew what "good girls" did. Actions speak louder than thoughts.

The child grew and became their willing sacrifice. It was all the child knew. Each one marched defiant, head down, resigned in defeat. Automatons with eyes wide shut.

The child died. It was all the child knew.

No one remembers the day Percy and Eve parted ways, but by its effects, they both assumed it had happened while the other wasn't looking.

This is the story of Percy.

This is the story of Eve.

This story would have had a very different ending if Percy and Eve had ever really met.

The End

We always see past something. It takes approximately .15 seconds from the moment the light hits our retina to when we have the earliest recognition of what we saw. Reaction time, no matter how rapid, is measured in time. An involuntary reaction like blinking takes .1 seconds to execute. Sound takes time to travel through the air. Information is transmitted from the past, filtered through the senses, and weighed and measured into memory.

A Constant Traveler Reminder:
CLEARING YOUR FILTER

Research cognitive biases. There are some interesting videos on YouTube that explain the basics.

Keep this in mind today: No matter how open minded we believe we are, we are subject to personal bias. We may be a clear filter, but we are a filter nonetheless.

30

An Elegant Mind Is Fore-giving.

It demonstrates that forgiving, like charity,
begins at home. It offers respect to
others before they meet.

*May you never forget what is worth remembering
nor ever remember what is best forgotten.*
—Irish blessing

Fore-giving is to offer in advance. It reframes the traditional view of overlooking error. It is a welcoming mind-set, an open door that offers friendship and acceptance in anticipation of meeting another. It also includes acceptance of your most intimate friendship—the one you have with your Constant Traveler, yourself.

If we don't respect ourselves, we are demonstrating that we don't know what respect is. How can we profess to respect anyone or anything? To establish this as my firm foundation, I must first cultivate self-respect.

If you don't respect yourself but profess to
respect another, is that respect or idolatry?

Regardless of whether we have offspring, we all are parenting a child. To live our best life, we must listen to our first and eldest child— the one inside—and offer him or her fore-giveness and respect.

UNLEASH
THE POWER OF THREE
I am here.
I see you.
I will stay.
Tell me more.
You are important.
I am listening.
Just be you.
You are enough.
I will share.
Just try it.
You are welcome.
You are loved.
I love you.

ACTIVATE
THE POWER OF TWO
If it is to be, it is up to *me.*

REALIZE
THE POWER OF ONE
I am you, and you are me.
We create our synergy.
All is well, we've found the sun.
Here together, *we are one.*

—PDT

A Constant Traveler Reminder:
KINTSUGI

There is a principle in Zen Buddhism called *kintsugi*, meaning golden joinery. It is the art of repairing that which is broken with gold lacquer. This practice, related to the concept of *wabi-sabi* in Japanese, teaches the practitioner to see beauty in the aged, flawed, and imperfect.

It arose from a perspective of functionality. When a piece of ceramic pottery was broken, instead of casting it onto the trash heap, it was repaired to continue its usefulness. Interestingly, the repairs were treated with gold. The vessel was repaired not to look as good as new but to emphasize and honor the repairs.

The concept of *kintsugi* symbolizes your intention to accept and live with your flaws and sorrows. You are invited to respect these, your most painful aspects and experiences, along with your most pleasurable learning experiences, because both have blended in a unique manner to become the unique and beautiful person that you are.

Repairing those broken vessels with great care, creativity, and attention, and mending them with one of the most valuable elements on earth is a potent teaching on the great value that can be mined from what seems, at the time, to be the parched, barren earth of your struggles and sorrows.

Approach the reparation of your traumas and sorrows with great care, creativity, and attention. Respect and

(continued)

honor the beauty of your brokenness. Use your memories as indicators of where you've been and as a means of showing you how far you have come. Let your flaws and sorrows serve you. Repair them with the most valuable emotion on earth: love.

FORE-GIVE YOURSELF A BREAK.
FORE-GIVE YOURSELF SOME LOVE...

My Blessing
I Bless my scars.
I Bless my wrinkles.
I Bless my age.
I Bless my eyes and ears and voice and heart and hands and feet.
I Bless my mind.
I Bless my life.
I Bless my mistakes.
I Bless my obstacles.
I Bless every morsel of food, every drink, every medication that I take into my body.
These blessings are clues so I can love better, listen deeper, speak wiser,
and live with elegance.
May my best life begin with my Blessing.

Bless your Blessings by sharing them...

31

An Elegant Mind Is Grateful.

It demonstrates that receiving is not taking.

One of the most precious gifts we can give our children is to teach them how to be grateful...

ELEGANT RECIPROCITY

It is as elegant (and perhaps more difficult) to receive with gratitude as it is to give from gratitude. Gratitude opens minds, but its gifts go much deeper. It sheds light on our vulnerable feelings of lack. This is expressed through our reluctance to acknowledge that we have needs. We protect our pain in this manner because we believe it indicates that we are somehow unsuccessful. It makes it impossible to accept assistance or to accept a gift without the intention of returning it.

YOU MAY NEED HELP YOURSELF, BUT DOES THAT MEAN YOU CANNOT HELP AS WELL AS RECEIVE IT?

To keep house plants vigorous and healthy, we must set up the conditions in which they thrive. We bring these plants into an artificial atmosphere and provide a finite amount of soil in which they may grow. It is up to us to allow them to flourish.

If we have provided the optimum environment, our plants keep growing and growing. In return for what we have given to them, they clean our air as well as make our rooms beautiful. Plants are live decorations. I am grateful for their beauty. And I am truly grateful to breathe clean air.

The relationship we create with plants is an example of the principle of reciprocity. We give them water and fertilizer and provide adequate light. They receive these and in turn give us clean air and beauty.

Giving and receiving, receiving and giving, like the concept of paying it forward, forms an inter-dynamic relationship that is symbolic of a circle. If there is a break in the circle, it cannot function as a circle. It is changed into something *other than* a give-and-take of energy that benefits both parties, and the relationship breaks down.

Given the proper conditions, the giver and the receiver immediately establish a relationship that is reciprocal—an interesting and challenging thought given that we have been taught that it is better to give than to receive.

IF EVERYONE INSISTS ON GIVING, WHO WILL THERE BE TO RECEIVE?

You know how it feels to give from your heart. You feel good, it feels right, you smile.... The act of giving leaves you with a residual feeling of well-being. You appreciate being able to give in such a manner, and you are deeply grateful for your personal bounty.

Over the years you have become conditioned to be suspicious of another person's offer. You feel there are strings attached, and many times there are. You have received at least one of those emails that informs you that a rich person in some foreign land has a fortune that needs to be deposited into your bank account to save it from the hands of those bent on that rich person's destruction. They offer you a significant portion as a reward for your kindness. You have been asked over and over for your hard-earned cash, had someone say, "If you are my friend, you will give me what I need." You feel preyed upon by those bent on taking what you have worked so hard to earn, and at the same time you beat yourself up for not extending this generosity. You have become jaded and wary of those bearing gifts.

Consider that same person with love in their heart (you or me) being asked to genuinely receive with the same intensity of feeling with which we freely give. You have also been taught that it is never good to be beholden. Society demonstrates to you that owing someone creates an obligation—it is the way that receiving works. To further your discomfort, consider what it would feel like if the person who wishes to give you something has significantly less to give than you do. You may feel compelled to say, "Oh. No, I'm good" or "You don't have to do that." You turn down the gift with as much graciousness as you can muster.

After you turn down a gift that is freely offered, how do you generally feel? Like you would have been taking from them? If you take their offering, then you are greedy, as if you are taking advantage of someone who does not have the resources to give you this gift. Or perhaps you don't value it because you have so much more or better than their meager offerings. Most times you don't see the interaction as being an energetic exchange, a barter, *an honorable swapping of value for value.*

151

Consider that perhaps the act of receiving triggers feelings of unworthiness in *you*. You protect your pain in this manner because to acknowledge it indicates that you are somehow unsuccessful, weak, that if you accept it, this proves you cannot provide for yourself what the other person is offering.

By not allowing another person to practice giving, are you not demonstrating your own belief in scarcity? *You* have observed the situation and decided that *they* will be less if they give away what they wish to give to you. *You* have decided that *they* need it more, so they should keep it for themselves. *You* don't need it. You who are conditioned to give are reluctant to acknowledge that you have needs. You have learned the art of polite refusal, to step around the giver with a smile and wave and to move on. You see this as a sign of strength, of independence, but inside you feel alone, and you suffer.

You don't want to be beholden. You don't want to enter into an agreement in which you are obligated to give anything back—and you really, truly believe that you will have to give something to them if you accept their gift.

COULD IT BE THAT DEEP INSIDE YOU FEEL IMPOVERISHED?

Your reluctance makes it impossible to accept a hand without considering it a handout. Your reluctance to receive makes it impossible to close the circle and feel the energetic flow that is the give-receive-give-receive flowing principle of reciprocity. And both parties lose.

Now consider the individual who wishes to give. How are they supposed to practice giving? How can they express to the world and confirm in their own lives that they have way more and are way more than enough if they cannot give away that which is theirs to give? How do they tap into the energetic flow of abundance and wash away their feelings of unworthiness and lack in those waters?

Consider the interactions of staff and the elderly residents in a nursing home. From society you are conditioned to see the helpless, vulnerable, dependent aspects of being elderly. These folks are clearly nearing the end of their lives. They cannot do what you can do any longer. Some cannot walk or speak, feed or clean themselves. Some have lost their minds to dementia. You see aging as deeply sad and scary.

There is another way of looking at this interaction—on the level of energy, of spirit. What if it is a genuine and loving energetic trade of value for value? What if the elegant, eternal minds that are now housed in elderly bodies are learning what it means to receive? What if the staff and volunteers with whom they interact—their caregivers—are being offered an opportunity to practice patience and kindness, to apply enthusiasm and good humor, to hone their skills in the elegant arts, to give of themselves as well as being offered gainful employment?

GRATITUDE IS THE COMMON GROUND.

The staff and volunteers are learning to give, and the elderly are learning to receive. Both are worthy. Both are necessary. It is the perfect place to observe the principle of reciprocity at work at a grassroots level.

A Constant Traveler Reminder:
COMMON ACTS OF GRATEFULNESS

How often have you expressed gratitude for the utilities and services you take for granted each day, such as your electricity, clean running water, your air-conditioning, and your heat? It is not enough that you pay for it—that can never be enough for an elegant mind. Enough is understanding and appreciating the profound gifts you enjoy every day in your home, the creature comforts that support your family, brought to your door by the teams of people who share their expertise and energy to make these services available.

Consider when the power goes out or when your car breaks down, has a flat, or runs out of gas on the highway. Consider when you get lost and have no cell service or when you are involved in an accident and need medical care and transportation. Consider when your beloved dog is sick, and you can't help her on your own. In those times, the expertise of those who provide the service you need is vital. How often do you gratefully offer these men and women your thanks? Or do you resent that their service didn't happen fast enough or well enough to save you from discomfort?

When your power service gets interrupted in the summertime (or for a short time in the winter), the outage is simply an inconvenience. The wintertime snow and ice storm outages add another level of concern, especially for those dependent on electricity for heat. Because of the expertise of these service men and women, you don't have that many outages in the span of a year; the power is on the majority of the time. It is easy to forget what an enormous privilege it is to have such consistent service. Millions of people in the world do not enjoy this level of comfort.

Offer a thank-you to the men and women who risk life and limb in 80-plus- as well as minus-30-degree temperatures and in hurricane and blizzard conditions so your family can have electrical power and clean running water and paved roads and ambulance services. The next time you go for a checkup or take your pet in for veterinary care, thank the doctor and staff. They deserve to know that you appreciate them for performing such vital community services.

32

An Elegant Mind Knows That No Thought Is So Important That It Cannot be Relinquished...

...if only for an instant.

THESE WRAITHS OF WRATH

And up they rise,
these wraiths of wrath
their point my weary mind assails.
And I, content, forgiveness paid,
trudge heavy laden t'ward my grave.

A whirling wind, my path is cleared,
its haunting dervish spinning wild.
I cast this taste upon you now
smothered sweet with guise and guile...

Behold its chasm, yawning wide
as vacant as such wind can be.
A paltry sum, this wrath of words,
scripted by the likes of me.

Begone! I whisper, sadly now...
I writhe in tendril's silent grasp.
Now free'd, they hone my destiny
as up they rise
these Wraiths of Wrath.

–PDT

"I think, therefore I am" is confusing, like a dog chasing its tail. I think, therefore I am, but what am I? I am what I think? Therefore, am I what I think I am?

I THINK, THEREFORE I SUFFER?

What is thinking? Is it not a compilation of experiences, facts, conclusions, and assumptions? It is stored as memory for instant access. *Stored, as in past tense.*

When you think, you suck the past through the present and project it onto your future. This is how you create your future. No wonder it sucks—you are never coming up with anything new. You lay an old template onto a new experience and experience the same poop in a different pile. You think you are creating a new pile, but like poop, it is a product of the past. The ego loves this mental excrement.

What is absolute about doubt? I doubt sometimes, and sometimes I don't. I am not always right; I am not always wrong—*that I do not doubt.*

Doubt is not a constant. Doubt is as random as your thoughts. *I am, therefore I am.* Now that has a ring to it....

The effort to maintain a solid and stationary platform has been costing you your life. It is why you grow old. Because you believe in the truth of your thoughts, you believe you are expressing your being. What if that is not so? What if your thoughts are not the expression of who you are but the indicator of your resistance to who you are?

TO TRULY SEE YOURSELF, YOU MUST BE CAPABLE OF LOOKING...

To understand thought, you must be willing to let go of your attachment to your personal perspective. You expend an extraordinary amount of life-force energy in your attempts to preserve the past and your definition of "what should be." That impulse shows up as a tightening, a quickening—your involuntary reaction to someone or something. This reaction is not the truth about them or it; it is merely your opinion.

Opinions are thoughts. Thoughts originate from somewhere. They are not the framework on which your world is constructed—*they are its decoration*. There is something deeper.

Your thoughts are deceptively contradictory and can change without a moment's notice. A well-constructed argument can change your mind about its topic forever. A startling bit of information can illuminate the darkest and most despairing thought. Thoughts are arbitrary, conceptive, and limited.

When you place your mind on something, you get drawn in. This creates a detail-oriented, progressively exclusive cascade of thoughts that begins to create a vision of that which you are thinking. You simultaneously include and exclude myriad options based upon your conditioning and past conclusions. You weigh and balance each bit of information—*it is not this, but that; it is not agreeable, but disagreeable; I like, I hate.* These solidify to become your present conclusion faster than the speed of light. So fast, in fact, that you do not recognize the subtle gap between your perception and its conclusion.

Place your attention in the gap. Otherwise you will never understand why you suffer.

A Constant Traveler Reminder:
DECORATING YOUR SANCTUARY

Another aspect of living in the gap is creation of a personal sanctuary. This can be an actual private space in your place of residence, but it is not limited to a physical space. It can also be a mind-full retreat that goes with you wherever you travel in life.

Use your imagination, and think of a relaxing place that you love. You can draw this image from anywhere—a beautiful picture you have seen or a place that represents safety and peace for you in life. Consider it with every sense that applies: how it looks, how it feels, how it tastes, how it smells, how it sounds.

Maybe it's your Gramma's kitchen, or a fishing hole, a cottage on a windswept beach, or a camp in the forest. Maybe it's your workshop. Maybe it's the space at home where you play your guitar, color with your child, or write poetry. Maybe you are sitting under an ancient pine tree at the top of an emerald green hill, gazing at the sparkling blue river below. There isn't a cloud in the sky, and the sun feels warm and relaxing on your skin. In the tree behind you, small birds twitter and coo. Breathe in the scent of pine. Listen to the whisper of the wind in its branches.

Your retreat will be unique and sacred to you. Think of it as a sanctuary tucked sweetly in your mind. Spend a few minutes experiencing every detail.

33

An Elegant Mind Realizes That Life Is for Living.

...not living for the things that clutter it.

ARE YOU FULL-FILLED?

There are many ways in which clutter takes over our lives. The most obvious is with material possessions. Even those heirlooms we consider so valuable may represent much more than our heritage.

WHEN IT COMES TO CLUTTER, WHAT WE GIVE AWAY
OR THROW AWAY MATTERS MORE IN LIFE
THAN WHAT WE KEEP...

De-cluttering our homes is only one aspect of living with an elegant simplicity. Barbara Hemphill of the Productive Environment Institute considers clutter postponed decisions. What decisions have you been putting off until tomorrow?

Let's consider some other ways that clutter takes over our lives:

Have you ever experienced what is termed the "blue screen of death" on your PC? Have you felt that sick feeling in your gut when you wonder if two years of work on that book you are writing or your collection of digital family pictures may have been lost? What if the classwork that took you a month to research and complete is now unrecoverable because you never got around to addressing those annoying messages about system errors or because you never got around to installing that anti-virus software?

When was the last time you went through your inbox and deleted the unnecessary emails or went through your photo file and arranged them so you can easily locate the ones you are looking for when you try to find them? Would you like to organize your office, file your papers, and work out a schedule for your precious time? When are you going to use that gym membership? Get that grinding sound in your car's front end examined? How many unfinished songs or poems or short stories or letters do you have in the works?

Consider that much of the stuff we keep isn't valuable or necessary or worthy of our maintenance. It doesn't serve any purpose. Living for the things that clutter our lives can also manifest as regret. My workbook, *Saving Your Own Life: Learning to Live Like You Are Dying*, is designed to assist you in feeling, dealing with, and healing your regrets.

Sometimes stuff = stuck. Stuff anchors you to permanence. It is a vignette to the past. Some call it nostalgia. In the olden days, the stuff that folks kept had a different meaning. It meant the difference between having enough provisions to get through a long, hard winter and starving to death. In our modern society, we have shopping centers and corner stores if we run out of something.

IN MODERN SOCIETY, PEOPLE STARVE TO
DEATH BECAUSE OF LACK OF COMPASSION,
NOT LACK OF RESOURCES...

Additionally, the black hole singularity that is consumerism is rapacious. Professional, psychology-based marketing tactics dictate what we need and what we cannot live without.

We do have a choice. We pay only if we pay attention to it.

A Constant Traveler Reminder:
BECOMING UNSTUCK

IF STUFF = STUCK, WHERE ARE YOU STUCK?

Perhaps you are stuck thinking about where you are stuck. Taking action rectifies that. Choose from the following categories, and begin to make a positive change:

Physical
Example: When was the last time you dedicated some time to making positive changes to your diet?

Social
Example: Have you often thought about widening your circle of friends or performing some form of community service?

Family
Example: Is there someone you know you need to talk to about something important but haven't done so because *this is the way it has always been?*

(continued)

Personal Development

Example: Have you been thinking for decades about joining a group (like Toastmasters) or taking a course (as in Tai Chi)?

Financial

Example: Do you have a short-term financial plan?

Career

Example: Have you developed a professional Standard of Excellence and held yourself accountable to it?

Spiritual

Example: Do you feel in touch with your personal creativity and Wellspring of Inspiration?

34

An Elegant Mind Appreciates the Prosperity of Others and Celebrates Its Own.

What is prosperity? Take a couple of minutes to consider your own definition. Where did your thoughts initially go when you were considering its meaning to you?

- Financial wealth and security
- Intelligence or education
- Relationships and family
- Physical, spiritual, and/or mental health
- Mother Nature's bounty and your own garden
- Your work
- Your hobbies and interests
- Your artistry
- The compassion of others
- Spiritual or philosophical domains
- Your country's riches and diversity
- Peace of mind
- The wonders of the Universe

Prosperity, the manifestations of abundance...

Prosperity is a proclamation of wholeness. It represents always having way more than enough in life. Not simply enough, but enough to share and celebrate as a demonstration of generosity in thought, word, and action. Prosperity and riches are known through their celebration!

A celebration is an acknowledgment of a gift or blessing. It is a declaration of possibilities as well as a process of completion. When we celebrate, we complete the circle of giving and receiving.

No person alive is exempted from their personal expression of abundance and its riches. We choose what we express by what we value. We express what we value by what we celebrate.

The flip side of abundance is manifest in many ways. We see it often in the envy or jealousy present in day-to-day competition. This happens as often on the world's stage as it does in private life. It is acted out in all stages of life.

A declaration...

What you envy (or are jealous of) in others becomes restricted in you. *That feeling is what restricted abundance feels like.* Feeling it is a declaration of that which you envy (or are jealous of) never happening in your life.

What you celebrate in yourself or in others flows unrestricted.

Energy is energy; it doesn't acknowledge difference. It demonstrates what you choose to express. Choose wisely.

A Constant Traveler Reminder:
CELEBRATE!

Become a Master of Celebration! What can you celebrate today? What is lovely? Thought-promoting? Joyful? Playful? Mysterious? Creative? Life-provoking?

You could begin by celebrating your breath. Life would be markedly different without it.

Share your discovery with someone else.

Celebrate like celebration is breath.
Celebration is the dance of the rich…

35

An Elegant Mind Understands That Without the Courage to Fail, It Will Always Fail to Succeed.

REFRAME FAILURE AND SUCCESS

When you decide that failure is not an option, you reframe it. *You* decide what success is and what failure is.

Consider the scientific model of trial and error. What marvelous accomplishments would have never been realized without the tenacity and process of failure? Failure to create something resulted in the discovery of something else:

- Penicillin
- The first practical implantable pacemaker
- The microwave oven
- Post-it Notes
- X-ray images

SUCCESS IS FAILURE REFRAMED...

Fearlessly pursue and discover your mission in life. Boldly go where no *you* has gone before. Be open to possibilities.

Become a success enthusiast as opposed to a failure avoider. It is impossible to forget about your failures, but it is entirely possible to shift your focus. If you can perceive choice, you can envision success. Simply choose again.

Your life will be reframed by your mission. When you have a purpose that is bigger than you, you let go of feelings of unworthiness. You are too focused on your pursuit to dwell on the past. You develop a thick skin and a keen ear—you welcome constructive criticism and pay no mind to destructive critiques.

INTENTION CREATES AND FORTIFIES ABILITY, WHICH LEADS TO OPPORTUNITY...

Ability is more than talent or knowledge. It is also enthusiasm, awareness, and gratitude.

Enthusiasm is infusing life with the high energy of our inspiration.

Awareness is learning to recognize opportunities and open doors.

Gratitude is celebrating and expressing our appreciation of what flows our way so as to attract more of the same.

SUCCESS IS...

- Standing up in a courageous manner.

- Gathering resources. Never ceasing to learn.

- Gathering support. Successful people demonstrate the value of connection by nurturing quality relationships.

- Anticipating the synergies and synchronicities of today.

- Being able to say, "Yes! I will pursue my best life because I deserve nothing less than the best!"

- Sharing your precious time and thoughts because they are worth sharing.

- Being able to say "no" when someone encroaches on your personal boundaries.

- Being willing to relinquish control of things beyond your sphere of influence.

- Having a well-developed and well-exercised sense of humor.

- Understanding that growth doesn't mean *expansion*, but it can mean *enrichment*.

- Pursuing quality experiences.

Success begins as a state of mind, so cherish your personal brilliance and realize what a magnificent gift it is. Never hide your brilliance. Be that shining example for whoever needs it. By doing so, you'll possess a mind-set focused on abundance and peace, the result of understanding that you are always more than enough.

ABUNDANCE IS THE FLOW OF INSPIRATION.
IT IS THE PRINCIPLE-BASED PURSUIT OF PROFITABILITY.
IT IS VALUE FOR VALUE...

The peaceful mind is free and uninhibited. It does not restrict the flow of inspiration.

Under these conditions, success as we understand it can manifest in a satisfying manner through these Five Steps for Success:

1. *Think* about it.

2. *Imagine* it, envision it. You *create* it in your personal Dream Theater like you are directing a movie.

3. *Speak* about it. Hear yourself *speak* it out loud.

4. *Feel* it happening right now.

5. *Behave* as if it is already yours.

A Constant Traveler Reminder:
REFRAMING SUCCESS AND FAILURE

How do you define success?

Where do you feel you have been successful?

If you were to describe how successful people define success, would it be different from your definition? Why?

How do you define failure?

Where do you feel you have failed?

If you were to describe how successful people define failure, would it be different from your definition? Why?

Name the greatest of all inventors. Accident.

—Mark Twain

36

An Elegant Mind Realizes That Abundance Is Attracted to Its Welcome.

Be happy with what you have, and you will
have plenty to be happy about.
—Irish proverb

If you wish for abundance, be grateful for what you have, and appreciate whatever you have. Gratitude and appreciation provide the welcome for more of the same. Gratitude transforms your vision. What you cannot recognize through self-concern now becomes clear.

WELCOME IS GRATITUDE EXPRESSED AS
APPRECIATION FOR A DREAM FULFILLED...

Never dwell on poverty unless you want more of it. Manifest the best by releasing the rest.

How to Grow Grass

The step-by-step process is as follows:

1. Climate: A consistent daytime and nighttime soil temperature is necessary for seed germination. If the temperature drops too low at night or is too high during the day, your seeding job won't work. Consult with a garden center in your area for optimum times to seed.

2. Soil: There must be nutrient-rich soil, approximately six inches in depth, to support a healthy root system. The soil cannot be hard and compacted; it must be loose and loamy for the tender sprouts to establish roots.

3. Moisture: There must be adequate, regular watering. This means watering twice daily (1/8 inch is enough to keep the seeds moist; more isn't necessary), *without missing a watering*, for a period of 14 days or until the seeds germinate.

4. Follow-through: Grass is quite resilient once it is established, but until that time, it requires a certain amount of ongoing care. Once the seeds have sprouted, consistent attention is important, as the sprouts still need watering until the roots become established.

Now that you are seeing green, your work isn't done—it's just begun. Germination and seedlings are not the end of the process. Barring excessive heat and drought, bugs, and natural disasters, you will grow grass. A lush, thick lawn is naturally weed resistant; however, weeds are opportunists. They have sustained themselves for eons due to their ability to adapt and take over anywhere they can find space. Expect to do some plucking or treating of the weeds that arrive in the middle of your seeding job. If you are patient, diligent, and follow this process, you can reasonably expect to have a nice lawn.

Seems simple enough, right? Miss one step in the process, and you won't have anything to show for your efforts.

Establishing the conditions that welcome abundance operates on these same principles.

Abundance is an attitude of anticipation and welcome. People who know abundance are receptive and passionate. They are confident in their personal worthiness, of being deserving of abundance, and are patient with the process in a manner that may surprise you. They do their best work, finish it to the best of their ability, and then let go of the outcome. Their patience comes from their ability to focus on another aspect of abundance instead of waiting for results to manifest. In this manner they are perpetually in a state of receptivity, of creative flow, and of welcoming.

The first step is to establish an achievable Passion Project. Think of a hobby or one of your interests that fires you up and ignites your passion-light—something that makes you feel energized when you consider it, something you may have desired to do for a long time. For your first project, pick something that takes effort but can be realized within a week.

CREATE YOUR WELCOME

Have faith in your potential (analogous to setting the climate for welcoming abundance):
- You must believe this is possible for you.
- You feel worthy and deserving of abundance.
- You feel grateful for what you have now (this is part of the perpetual state of receptivity and the quality of your present practice).
- Motivate yourself! Have a clear understanding of why you desire this goal and *why* it is important to you.

• You are willing to not only *give* what it takes to succeed (effort, finances, time), but more importantly, you are ready and willing to *receive* what it takes to succeed. It is vital to review your beliefs surrounding both giving and receiving.

Gather material resources (analogous to nutrient-rich soil): What do you need for this goal to be achieved?
• Physical well-being and vitality
• Finances
• Credentials, licenses
• Permits, applications
• Education, training
• Space (rental or owning property)
• Materials, product, inventory, and equipment

Shower it with attention (analogous to consistent moisture):
• Reinforce your faith in abundance with regular, consistent, passionate attention.
• Create a schedule and reminders so you stay on track. You will refer to it often.
• Revisit your "Why?" regularly. Your willingness to go the distance will be a challenge to your endurance and commitment to this goal.
• Establish dates to periodically reevaluate your commitment, reexamine your motivation, and adjust as necessary.

Cultivate patience (unrealistic expectations can sabotage your goal):
This is where many a worthy goal becomes a victim of sabotage. You may create obstacles to your success if you do not experience the progress you expected and become frustrated, or if success is not coming fast enough to keep you from becoming discouraged.

It is good at this point to examine your expectations. Are they based on real-life circumstances? Another aspect to consider is that your circumstances are unique. Other people's timelines for success or failure may not correlate with yours, particularly if you have very few examples with which to work. This is a case of what is called in psychology survivor bias—when you are more apt to focus on those who succeed over those who did not due to the survivor's visibility. However, the higher the percentage of people who have accomplished something within a set time frame, the greater the likelihood that it will work in the same manner for you.

Let go of the outcome (a lesson from Stephen King):

Stephen King is one of the world's most successful and prolific writers. In his book *On Writing*, he describes how he creates a new manuscript draft and then puts it aside for an extended period, not looking at it again until that time is up. He consciously lets it go and turns his mind to his next project. When he does return to this project, he does so with new eyes.

This is instruction in letting go of a project as well as it is an elegant lesson in remaining in the flow of inspiration. King does not allow himself to get bogged down by one project. He does not interrupt the flow of inspiration. He does not get weighed down by the details of this one and miss out on the next wonderful supernatural tale that he knows is waiting for him, *because he knows that there is more where that came from.*

It is easy to get so absorbed in one project that it takes on a life of its own and, like a demon or succubus, takes over our life, very much like the plot of one of King's horror novels! The author has learned the art of letting go of his creations to free up space for the abundance of fresh possibilities and new creation. He knows that new is now.

Welcome your abundance

Here are some aspects of abundance that you may wish to try on in your own life:

• Do excellent, ethical work that represents the very best you have to offer.

• Put it out there with confidence. Let no person or circumstance inhibit your brilliance.

• Prepare for success. Envision a plan for when it happens—feel it in your bones. Live as if it is arriving today.

• Keep the creativity flowing. Move on to the next project with passion, enthusiasm, and excellence!

The order of operations:

Passion Project 1
  • Polish your performance—do your best work.
  • Present your work properly.
  • Plan and prepare for success.
  • Presume a positive outcome.
  • Practice patience—let go of this project.
    Remain in a state of receptivity.

Passion Project 2...

A Constant Traveler Reminder:
CREATE A PASSION PROJECT

Pick a Passion Project that can be achieved within one week. Apply what Stephen King recommends.

37

An Elegant Mind Delights in Good Humor.

It demonstrates that funny is now,
happiness is now, laughter is now.

If you lose the power to laugh, you lose the power to think.
—Clarence Darrow

There is more than one way to live in the present moment,
but humor is the very best method imaginable.

HUMOR IS NOW THERAPY...

When you find something truly funny, you are irresistibly
and gently drawn into the present moment. When you laugh,
you are finding something funny now, not yesterday or tomorrow. Consider how great it feels to belly laugh to the point
where you are totally helpless. That wonderful, relaxed feeling is
an expression of what it means to live in the now.

THIS IS SERIOUS PLAY...

This is not the satire, sarcasm, or degrading humor that often passes for funny. This is not laughing at someone's expense. For me, this is Tim Conway and Harvey Korman funny; Robin Williams and Jonathan Winters funny; Bill Murray, Julie Bowen, Sofia Vergara, Jim Carrey, Will Ferrell funny. Good-humored, outrageous silliness guaranteed to delight any person who is young at heart.

One of the indicators of depression is the inability to laugh. Sometimes a person is so overwhelmed by thoughts of their difficult past and fear-filled future that their present has no room for laughter. Humor is healing medicine. Hearty laughter relieves stress and relaxes the body for up to 45 minutes afterward. It also boosts the immune system. That is why sick people are sometimes prescribed watching funny movies as part of their therapy.

A good laugh and a long sleep are the two best cures for anything.
—Irish proverb

A Constant Traveler Reminder:
LAUGHTER FOR WHAT AILS YE

Laughter connects people. It is a gift. It relieves stress and creates contentment and calm.

Feeling lonely?
Invite a friend over to watch a silly movie.
Start a book group.

Attend a comedy at the movie theater.

Visit a dog park.

Join an improv acting group.

Organize a night of activities that celebrate the kid in you!

Here are some activity-night suggestions to help get the ball rolling. Now just because there's a label on these for women, men, or coed, it doesn't mean you have to stay within your own gender to enjoy them. Who knows what kind of fun you may have if you try something out of the ordinary?

FOR WOMEN:

Girls Night
- The hostess selects a girly movie
- Take turns doing each other's nails
- Each person brings their own mask/facial product (can be purchased cheaply at a drug store)
- Additional activity: a cheap craft of some kind
- Potluck: pizza and popcorn

Musical Chairs
- A grown-up version of a child's tea party!
- Hostess selects a musical-based movie

Suggestions: *Mamma Mia!, Chicago, Moulin Rouge, Les Misérables, Burlesque, The Sound of Music*, or animated selections like *Frozen, The Princess and the Frog*, or *Moana*

- Pick from a selection of herbal teas (each guest, bring one). Drink tea and enjoy (preferably healthy) sweets!

Suggestions: angel food cake, flavored light-sugar yogurt, and fresh berries   (continued)

- Frozen yogurt and sprinkles
- Fruit kebabs dipped in dark chocolate
- Frozen yogurt grapes
- Coconut yogurt, blueberry, and granola parfaits
- Avocado brownies
- Watermelon pizza
- Chocolate-dipped fruit cones
- Grilled peaches with cinnamon and honey

Kid Night
- Hostess selects a sweet or funny movie
- Each guest brings their jammies for relaxing
- Each guest brings a coloring book, crayons, colored pencils, or markers and stickers
- Menu is microwave popcorn for the movie, PB&J sandwiches, or PB&Banana, or Pizza and beverage

FOR MEN:

Gadget Night/Video Game Tournament
- Host selects the video game and gets the prize for the winner
- Each guest brings a gadget or something interesting to let the others try
- Potluck: burgers or pizza and beverage (each guy brings something)

Board or Card Game Night
- Host selects the game (or games). Host purchases steak for the winner to take home as their prize. Suggestions: Texas Hold 'em, Crib, Rummoli, Gin Rummy, UNO, Crazy 8s

- Potluck: same foods as above or select another easy option like beans & weiners, or hot dogs (can be vegan!)

Action/Adventure or Sport Night

- Host picks favorite action or adventure movie or sporting event
- Dart game before or after the movie/sporting event
- Each guest brings a box of frozen prepared chicken wings; burgers, onions, cheese, and buns; or sausages, mustard, sauerkraut, and buns

FOR MEN, WOMEN, OR COED:

Something Silly Night

- Host picks a funny movie or cartoons; or organizes a Crazy 8 tournament
- Each person is responsible to contribute to the Happy! Happy! Happy! meal: Food with faces (like you make for kids—check online for examples); small pizzas with salami faces, olive eyes, and green pepper smiles; cupcakes with Smarties for eyes and grins; banana splits, M&Ms, hot dogs, or burgers
- Each person finds a really funny joke (or jokes) that *you could tell to a young teenager to share with the others*
- Balloons!!!

38

An Elegant Mind Realizes That We Always Act in a Manner That Pleases Us...

...even if that manner causes us pain.

Back in the early '90s I worked as a receptionist for a large industrial company. It was part of my duties to call the manager of the department when the person with whom they were meeting showed up, to announce that they had arrived.

One morning a casually dressed man came in, asked for one of our managers, and took a seat to wait. I called the manager and while we were waiting for him to come and retrieve his guest, the guest and I struck up a conversation.

You know—niceties like "Nice day out there." We may have discussed who was winning the latest sports series...just a few ritualized words to pass the time...

Nobody else arrived at reception and the switchboard was quiet. As the conversation progressed, we began talking about education.... I mentioned something about my beginning in a performing arts degree program at university a while ago and quitting. I said that I had the chance, but now it was too late...I had a young family now and a job...obligations. I told him, with a wry smile, that I let that opportunity slip away.

I expected him to shake his head, smile, and agree—after all, he didn't know me and in the next few minutes he would be gone...never to be seen again.

But it was then that the conversation changed. This guy got serious, and a bit frustrated with me.

"I don't believe that for a second," he said in a firm tone, his eyes on the floor. "You can go back anytime you want. If you really want it, that is, you will find a way."

His emotional response stopped me cold. I had inadvertently struck a nerve. Perhaps he had struggled with this same dilemma at some point in his career...maybe repeated these same words?

Stunned into silence, I struggled to shift gears. It was my job to be nice to guests, not to tick them off!

At that moment the manager we were waiting for arrived. Without a second glance the guy got up and walked out of my life.

He genuinely confused me that day. However, with years of trekking on the path of life behind me, combined with my memories of skinned knees and stepping in slimy stuff, I now understand his words.

Mister Whoever-you-were, thank you. I have never forgotten you or your words of wisdom shared in those loaded seconds back in what was probably 1992, even if they were delivered with frustration and you most likely didn't give them a second's thought after you delivered them.

I heard you.

Thank you, sir, for caring enough to speak. You didn't waste your breath.

COMMON ELEMENTS

Where is your sacred?
Is this it?
If you expand your life
to stretch
from the moment you came to life
until the
moment you depart life,
does that offer you
the
stuff of dreams?

Of inspiration?

Of mystery?

If you accept the mystery as religion,
you will be challenged.
If you accept the mystery as science,
you will be challenged.
Do you accept these common elements?

What can be adequately
described,
accepted, or
rejected
by what it
isn't?

You believe
you've made
a choice...

You can live a life of
combat and opposition.
There is no one or
no thing that can stop
you.

If someone were to restrain
your arms and legs
and hold you down,
still,
they cannot stop you.
Is that what you call
freedom?

You can offer
contempt and derision
for those
who engage the mystery on
purely
religious terms.

You can offer
contempt and derision
for those
who engage the mystery by
purely
scientific means.

Do you accept these common elements?

Have you not
sworn allegiance
to
a life of opposition,
locked in
mortal combat
with what you
are not?

Is that it?

Friend, what are you?

Are you defined by
what
you
oppose?

Where is your sacred?

Surely even
your enemies
hold something
sacred,
if nothing else
it is
you.

Surely you
hold something
sacred,
if nothing else
it is
your enemy.

Those who have
enemies
will always
find them.

What you value,
you demonstrate.

You live your values.

What you honor,
you express.

You live your honor.

What you respect,
you live.

You live your Way.

What you hold sacred,
you believe.

You live your sacred.

You live
your version
of
freedom
when you
deny
another
theirs.

You live
your lies, or
you live
your
truth.

What say you now?

This *is* your
challenge.

This *is* your
mystery.

This *is* your
sacred.

Do you accept these common elements?

—PDT

How to Nurture a Life of Privilege

1. Accept your enrollment in the School of What Is.

It comes as a gift along with your birthday. Want to be something? Be a model student.

The School of What Is has one textbook. No one wrote it. Nobody owns it. It has two chapters, no specifics:

- Chapter 1. Life, aka The Now
- Chapter 2. Death, aka The End

These are yours to discover, because this school is self-directed. You experience the details and record them for yourself.

2. Rock your wise.

Embrace the beauty and simplicity of your elegant mind.

3. Life is made up of both light and dark matter.

Sometimes life sucks. You get sick. You fall. Folks die. You die. Your good ol' dog dies. You get wrinkled up and feel terrible.

Lean into it. Feel your pain, don't suppress it—hunker down and live through it. Learn from it, and move along.

4. Don't be anyone's victim. They can't make you be.

You don't have to merely survive; you can learn how to thrive. Thriving is reasonable. If you don't have a clue how to do it, find someone you respect who is thriving, and ask them.

5. You are no different from anyone else.

Every human gets caught in the mire. Tragic stories are like bellybuttons—everyone has at least one.

Rewrite the story of you. Shift genres from tragedy to triumph—talk about that. Let what you've learned while in the mire inspire others to be like you—*one of the cool kids.*

6. Become a master of appreciation.

Abolish the shoulda, coulda, wouldas. They are theories. Kick their sorry asses to the curb, and live practically.

7. Nobody owes you anything for anything.

Breathe in. Breathe out. Repeat.

8. Live elegantly.

Hashtag passion! Live each day with your unique artistic flair. Never hide your brilliance. Look for others who shine, and run with that crew.

9. Choose kindness.

Kindness applies to everyone, most especially you. Share it like you are teaching the world how to do it.

10. Polish your mirror. Clean that glass every day.

Keep your mind open so you can see how your energy is being reflected back to you, and learn from it.

11. Question everything.

Consider deliberately. Do not accept or reject anything on impulse or as directed by fear.

12. Love.

Love + Life = Logic.

Life is a vibe (gotta love those quantum folks!).

Love is the highest vibe.

13. Live like that.

Oh, and there may be a Tea Party at the end…

A Constant Traveler Reminder:
LIVE LIKE THAT

Do you enjoy your privileges? What privileges are you enjoying at this very moment? Choose as many as apply:
- I showed up today, on this side of the grass.
- I have taste and sight and hearing and feelings.
- I get to eat good food and drink clean water.
- I am cool enough or warm enough.
- I am safe.
- I can choose who I love.
- I can love my children, my partner.
- I can appreciate beauty and art.
- I can show others where to look for love, beauty, and art.
- I can listen and talk.
- I can grow and learn.
- I can be kind.
- I can do *Everything Gently.*
- I have hands and feet and brains and heart to do my work.
- I can offer the world my "grinny face."
- I can dance (even if I think I can't).
- I can laugh.
- I can play.
- I can explore.
- I can make course corrections.

- I can bend.
- I can be elegant.
- I can begin again.
- I can _____ (feel free to add your own)
- I can _____
- I can _____
- I can _____

For whoever you meet this day, be their inspiration...

How can you be of service? Serve this moment. Put some soul into it! The world is waiting for you.

39

An Elegant Mind Is Comfortable with Discomfort.

It knows that we cannot avoid our pain if we truly wish to transcend it.

OUR FEAR OF DEATH HAS PUT FEAR IN ITS PLACE, AND FEAR MAKES A NASTY TRAVELING COMPANION. THIS IS THE ULTIMATE DISCOMFORT...

The fear we feel is in relation to the loss of the self-infused body. What would happen if we withdrew our focus from ourselves?

Muscles grow through resistance, not comfort. Comfort leads to stagnation.

We live in a world where pleasure and comfort are considered the ultimate luxuries. Truth is, when we have it easy, we are not motivated to learn or grow. There are people who make a living out of avoiding discomfort. That sometimes takes more energy than addressing the discomfort once and for all.

FEAR, NOT DEATH, IS THE ENEMY OF LIFE

Why do we so often wage war? Because we know our enemies better than we know ourselves...

The most effective way to address our fear of death is to embrace our life-sucking fear with relentless compassion and gentle vigor. We find these qualities when we begin to dig deep inside ourselves, when we turn to face this enemy, *because they who have enemies will always find them.*

We fear the unknown. We fear the future. That we fear a very personal and unknown future is also the reason for the fear in the first place.

We cannot understand this enemy if we cannot examine it any more than we cannot see beyond a brick wall to what is on the other side. If we were to consider our fear a brick wall, we would begin to understand that we have become our own jailors.

With that in mind, we have a choice. We can face our discomfort and become fearless—bit by bit become *more and more comfortable with feeling the discomfort of our thoughts* to handle the bricks composed of fear and begin to dismantle the wall, or we can *resist what sucks and remain stuck.*

FOCUS ON FEAR: BECOME A MASTER OF DEMOLITION

We all know what happens after birth. We live our precious life. However, even after eons of searching, we have no proof of what happens after death and are deeply afraid of it.

How do we begin to accept the reality of death that we all face? Embrace today. Be as ready to "live it" as you are to "kill it" or "crush it."

Death is a concept. That is obvious, as you are not yet dead. Once you are dead, death is a concept no longer. Death seems like the easy part—it will take care of itself regardless of your compliance or non-compliance. It is the events and thoughts about those events leading up to your demise that generate the fear and build the wall. It is also the events and the thoughts about those events leading up to your death that can make or break *your life*.

Consider that wonderful night in 1989 when the whole world celebrated the demolition of the Berlin Wall. The image of a piece of that wall below says it all.

Section of the Berlin Wall, with art by Indiano,
Imperial War Museums, London.

Face your thoughts one by one. That is manageable. Grasp them with passion and vigor, and rattle them until they shake loose from the wall. Focus on each with intensity. If you fall during the demo process, which we all do, be ready to take what comes. *Be set to fall forward....*

Each brick in the wall represents the blocked energy within you. Relentless focus shakes the bricks loose, allowing the energy to flow. Celebrate each small triumph. Use what works (what empowers and energizes you), and keep doing it until it no longer works. Revise your plan and continue.

A Constant Traveler Reminder:
ATTENDING TO REGRETS

The Top Five Regrets of the Dying, as outlined by palliative care nurse, Bronnie Ware, in her book *The Top Five Regrets of the Dying—A Life Transformed by the Dearly Departing*, offers us a chance to address and resolve the regrets that hold us back from living our best life.

1. I wish I'd had the courage to live a life true to myself, not the life others expected of me.
2. I wish I hadn't worked so hard.
3. I wish I'd had the courage to express my feelings.
4. I wish I had stayed in touch with my friends.
5. I wish that I had let myself be happier.

Consider which of the areas noted that require your attention.

If you have a legal will, make sure it is up-to-date. If you don't have a will, perhaps it is time to begin the process of creating one. My workbook, *Saving Your Own Life: Learning to Live Like You Are Dying*, addresses these items and more.

You must step out of your comfortable rut in order to find your personal groove…

40

An Elegant Mind Recognizes the Value of What It Is to Be Human.

It realizes that skinned knees and bruises are part of its incredible journey.

IF THE EXPERIENCE IS THE REWARD,
CAN YOU LIVE WITH THAT?

To realize the profound gift of being born human, we must first realize it as something to be valued. We have the unique ability, among all beings with which we share this planet, to think and discover new things and to apply what we have discovered. We have the awareness that there is more to life than what we see. We can choose again.

We can truly grasp the meaning of suffering. We may slip in the slimy stuff and fall, skinning our knees, but we have the presence of mind to pick ourselves up, clean our shoes, and move on. The difference between us and less-evolved beings is that we hold the potential to learn from our suffering and transcend it. Human beings are hardwired for transcendence.

WE ARE ALL IN THIS TOGETHER...

We can develop empathy by our understanding that suffering is a universal condition. We can acknowledge our own pain and appreciate the long and rocky road we have traveled to get to where we are today. We can bring this understanding to life and relate it to others by extending compassion for their struggles. As far as we can determine, no other living being can come to these realizations. Theirs is continuous struggle, as they exist at a level that does not allow for the *awareness of transcendence*.

Sometimes we forget that we are living a gift, and we get sucked into the mire. We despair and behave like less-evolved beings. To return to our elegant mind takes compassion. It must first fill the mind and heart of the one offering it—we must forgive ourselves for our mistakes by realizing that we do better once we know better.

What is it that we offer one another each day? Is it the best of us? Do we offer value for value?

DON'T UNLOAD YOUR PAINFUL LIFE EXPERIENCES
ON OTHERS. WHEN YOU SHARE, MAKE IT ABOUT HOW
YOU'VE GAINED, NOT HOW YOU'VE BEEN PAINED...

A Constant Traveler Reminder:
STEP INTO THE CHALLENGE

When faced with a challenging situation, follow the steps outlined below:

Step 1. Identify the challenging issue (be specific).
Is this issue within my power to influence (can I influence the outcome)? If you say, "No, I do not have control over this situation, event, project, person, etc.," then practice letting go. (To begin, check out these articles on the website PsychologyToday.com):
- "Let It Go!"
- "How to Let It Go"
- "Important Tips on How to Let Go and Free Yourself"
(See: *The Four Agreements* by Don Miguel Ruiz)
If you can say, "Yes, my choices here can have significant influence on the outcome," then clarify the issue using the tools of an investigative reporter, asking the who, what, when, where, why, and how questions (see below).

Remind yourself: *I may not have the ability to control the situation, but I do have the ability to control my thoughts about it and to gain and maintain my cool.*

Step 2. Establish a desired outcome. Make it simple and direct.

Step 3. Form a plan.
Use your imagination. Brainstorm two or three possible

(continued)

options. (Be creative. You may wish to enlist the help of a resource person, trusted friend, or mentor.)

Step 4. Consider the pros and cons. List as many as you can for each option. (Utilize your resource person, friend, or mentor if necessary.)

Step 5. Choose one option. Decide on the best possible plan of action.

Step 6. Take the step. Act according to your plan.

Step 7. Monitor results and feedback.
Did this plan work well? If yes, then continue using this method.

If no, then there is room for improvement, so learn from this experience. Make adjustments as necessary, and apply what you have learned to your next challenge.

Step 8. Find the best possible solution. Learning new behavior is an ongoing process. Continue to monitor results and adjust accordingly.

Here's how an investigative reporter would handle the situation:

1. <u>Who</u> is involved? *Who* can I bring in to help me as resource people?

2. <u>What</u> are the facts? *What* would happen if I do not find a solution?

3. <u>When</u> did this challenge arise? *When* does it need to be resolved?

Determine the urgency and importance of the issue. If it is not a crisis, then clarify the time frame in which you have to act. Wherever possible, the wise choice is to give yourself time to make the wisest possible choice. Give it a day or two (or maybe more). Keep in mind that many times clarity and perspective are gained once the issue sits with you for a while. Take the time you need. Don't let anyone pressure you, not even you.

4. <u>Where</u> did it happen? *Where* will I feel the effects of this challenge?

5. <u>Why</u> do I need a solution? *Why* is it important?

6. <u>How</u> can I find out more? *How* will my life be different when I find a solution? *How* can I involve resource or support people?

41

<u>An Elegant Mind Knows That Everyone Has Suffered Loss...</u>

...and that although they may not remember, everyone has been touched by love.

JUST FOR TODAY

I will lay down my sword.
Just for today,
I'll relinquish old sores, if
just for today.
I stand here, determined,
there's no other way.
I'll walk in the sunshine, if
just for today.
Just for today
I'll lead with a smile.
Just for today
I'll let go for a while, if
just for today.
And I won't turn away,

share my heart with another, if
just for today.

Just for today,
may each step that I take,
take me somewhere more lovely,
if just for today.

—PDT

THIS IS YOUR STORY...

E veryone has a story. You have felt less than. You have cried the hot, bitter tears of loss. You have felt the fingers of sickness and death in your life. You have felt that surge of darkest outrage when you see injustice and misery.

An aspect of compassion is to offer empathy for those who suffer. In this way you acknowledge the universality of the suffering of all living creatures, because you acknowledge your own pain. This empathy is what can bring people together on a level that even the most skilled mediator cannot.

Sometimes it seems that your entire life has been marked by hardship, sadness, and suffering. Most likely it has not *always* been this barren, but there are times when you cannot see past it. You look around in desperation and do not see love anywhere.

You can create your own soft place to fall. You can provide for yourself the things that a nurturing mother as well as a guiding, protective father would provide.

It is important to remember that regardless of what the world has shown you up until this point, you have been touched by the form of love that is life. You are part of this outstanding tapestry that is being delivered into each moment with an astonishing surety. *You have your place in this puzzle simply by coming to life. It* was not reserved for you by anyone else—it has been yours all along. It is up to you to live it.

Can you appreciate your contributors—those who have helped set the conditions for you to come to life? Can you give yourself the support and encouragement that a good mother and a good father would give to you?

A Constant Traveler Reminder:
SHARE YOUR TIME

Search for volunteer services in your area and offer your time to a cause that interests you. It can be as little as an afternoon or as much as you can find time to invest in. With this exercise, the key is that you must physically show up and make your contribution. Volunteering has the ability to change your life if you are willing to explore that possibility.

42

An Elegant Mind Offers an Opinion Only After Thoughtful Deliberation.

As one piece of a grand jigsaw puzzle, it realizes it cannot grasp how all the pieces fit together.

If we were supposed to speak more than we hear, then we'd have two mouths and only one ear. —Mark Twain

A very wise bunny once said, "If you can't say something nice, don't say nothin' at all." Yep, Thumper knew stuff.

A person whose mind is focused on elegance offers his or her opinion only after thoughtful deliberation. This person knows that they cannot possibly grasp the whole picture. They have learned self-control, and so they do not react to provocation. When something (a thought, situation, or event) hooks their attention, they abstain from responding until they have thought it through from the perspective of being able to offer something beneficial to all concerned. And when they do offer their thoughts, they lead with the statement that this is merely their opinion, not the "gospel" according to any man or woman.

However, once their words are spoken, they stand by what they say in an honorable way. Being a person of principles, they do not go back on their word. Additionally, they allow the other person (or persons) the freedom to think otherwise without attack or judgment.

This is the sign of a mature spirit. Knowing when to speak (or comment) and when to remain silent is an art as well as a virtue.

THE GOOD OPINIONS OF OTHERS

The person who feels confused about their life due to the opinions of others has given those others their personal power. If you are a people pleaser, you totally get it. You also understand that when someone says, "Don't give a shit what others think," it doesn't help one bit. Words do have the *potential* to hurt you—both what others say to you and *what you say in return.*

Can you admit that you are tied to the opinions of others, to the acceptance of the group, to that degree? Perhaps it is a matter of conditioning. Perhaps you have never seen demonstrated, in an impactful manner, what an autonomous, decisive, free-thinking individual looks and sounds like. Perhaps you have been deeply influenced by a group that is governed by strict laws, rituals, and routine. People who are comfortable with blending in and not standing out. People who are deeply afraid of individual expression.

You may imagine a different life, one in which you are free to think differently from the collective, but you get shut down and/or rejected when you offer your thoughts. You feel the force of the group's condemnation in this tentative attempt at individual expression, and it is too much. You feel powerless on your own and attempt to comply. You do not understand that you have unconsciously sacrificed your autonomy (personal power) to the collective and have agreed to draw power from the group in the manner that it dictates is appropriate.

Most times, attempting to comply does not work, as it only

serves to make you more and more unhappy. It can, in the mind of the thinker, become a matter of life and death—a slow, sleep-walker's death due to being smothered by mundane, regimented, conformist thoughts.

There is a difference between thinking for yourself and opposing conformity. The former does not involve resistance or anger. It involves doing the inner work to understand your-self and your motives and then applying what you understand with intention in an assertive manner. Take, for your example, Mahatma Gandhi. Learn about yourself, and become clear on what you truly stand for. Set a clear intention, and refuse to allow others to sway you when you are acting from your inspiration.

Create a clear vision. Set your attention on attracting the good stuff. Then rock your life!

A Constant Traveler Reminder:
THINK TWICE, SPEAK ONCE

If you were welcoming a person you highly respected (but had never met) into your home, would you begin your conversation by complaining about everything you felt was wrong about your life, point out everything they should change in their life, and recount every horrible action that you have witnessed in the world?

Would you not wish to provide your esteemed guest with the very best that you have to offer?

We may not aspire to be master teachers, but we are an example for someone...

(continued)

Before responding, it is beneficial to keep in mind the following:

Not everything I think is helpful.

Not everything I say is wise.

Not everything I do contributes to my well-being or to the well-being of those around me.

There is an adage used in the carpentry trade: Measure twice, cut once. In this manner the carpenter doesn't waste wood. Fine cabinetry is reflective of the thoughtful patience that goes into it.

Beginning today, *think twice, speak once.* Whatever you do today, make your contribution with tact and elegance. By this simple gesture, you save your breath and offer respect by not wasting another's time.

43

An Elegant Mind Maintains a Tranquil Disposition.

It is not prone to drama.

ALIVE IN THE GAP...

We all appreciate that friend who is always the same. She is trustworthy, reliable, solid, and stable. She doesn't over-react. She doesn't let circumstances or whim dictate her mood. This friend chooses her attitude and demonstrates the benefits of living in the gap, having diligently practiced during times of mundane as well as high emotion. She understands that erratic behavior and excessive reactions are generally problematic for her as an individual as well as for everyone she encounters.

Consider how pleasant it is to be around this relaxed, easy-going person. You can always rely on her to offer a reasonable, supportive, well-considered point of view. You are grateful to know her. This person, by her presence in your life, teaches you to *rock your wise* and realize the benefits of a tranquil mind.

Through her example, you are invited to:

- Realize that dramatic personality highs and lows are indicative of imbalance and suffering. They are signposts to what needs to be addressed.

- Utilize provocation as a prompt for you to be calm.

- Understand that the extreme high cannot be maintained and that the extreme low cannot last.

- Become slower to take offense, thoughtful in action, and deliberate in speech.

- Identify your tendencies and triggers and choose beforehand to never attack through thought, word, or action.

- Hold silence as sacred by reserving the right to use it.

- Accept personal responsibility for actions with an even temper.

- Offer graceful acquiescence for what you cannot change.

- Consistently apply the four Fs of effective action: *fearless faith, focus, and fortitude.*

- Realize that thoughtful deliberation leads to no regrets.

- Endeavor to live according to your present means and immediate circumstances.

- Understand the value of living in the gap.

Perspective is space, and this is realized in the gap between provocation and action. It can also be called deliberation.

Wisdom is realizing the value of perspective.

A Constant Traveler Reminder:
BREATHWORK

Life is wind. As a demonstration, hold your breath for 30 seconds. Knowing how to breathe (the most powerful person in the room is the one with the most relaxed breathing pattern) is a vital life practice.

Widening the Gap with 4x4
Practice mindful breathing. This short and simple 4x4 technique can be utilized anywhere:

1. If you feel comfortable doing so, place your hand on your stomach, and concentrate on expanding your abdomen in the inhale and contracting your abdomen on the exhale. This is called belly breathing.

2. If you are standing, feel your feet on the ground and your solid, strong stance. If you are sitting, feel your sit bones, back against the chair, and feet solidly planted.

(continued)

3. Inhale through your nose to the count of 4, hold to the count of 4, and slowly exhale through your mouth to the count of 4. Counting helps you concentrate and take your mind off the situation or thought.

4. Really keep track of time, give yourself permission to let go of stress, and allow yourself to relax.

Continue these for 4 repetitions, then return to your regular breathing pattern.

There are many wonderful breathing techniques available online. Research other breathing practices, as you may wish to incorporate them into your daily practice. Dr. Andrew Weil, MD, offers many exercises and techniques on his website, www.drweil.com.

44

An Elegant Mind Is an Open Mind.

It allows for a free flow of thoughts and does not attach itself to them. It does not attack itself or others with judgment, condemnation, or guilt.

WARRIOR

A Warrior, she's often been,
obsessed with other lands.
In tending to her freedom, so
content to raise her hand.
Yet even in the midst of war,
surrounded and alone
she knew t'was might that brought her here,
and sliced her to the bone.

This Warrior has sheathed her sword.
Its glint may dull, at will.
Her wounds, now tender'd, body bathed.
Her feet now soft and still.
All wagers off, she's settled in,
sworn enemies released and whole.
Old Warrior, the time is nigh
to find yourself at home.

—PDT

I am happy to say that I am a Canadian. Canada is a cultural mosaic, a country founded on the inclusion of myriad cultures, genders, and ethnicities. We have made some mistakes in the past, particularly with our First Nations people, but we are working toward remedying these errors as a collective.

I grew up in the rural community of Cassilis in the province of New Brunswick. I went to a small, one-room school in my community until 1970, when that school was closed. I knew everyone in my school. I knew everyone in my community. The only time I interacted with strangers or folks I didn't know was when I went to church.

I was raised Roman Catholic, and our church was located at the end of the Red Bank bridge, on the Metepenagiag Mi'kmaq Nation reserve in Red Bank. I went to church with Indigenous people, and from age 11 on, I went to school with Indigenous kids, but it wasn't until I was in my 50s that I truly began to understand the racism that these people have had to endure—not just in that community, but all over Canada and the United States.

I was not taught about what really happened to Indigenous people in our Canadian-history class in school. At that time, many Indigenous children my age were growing up in *residential schools*. I grew up safe in my own home on the Cassilis road, a privilege my counterparts in the residential schools did not have. That is a tragedy beyond description.

Now we, as a nation, have been given a glimpse of what those children and young people endured. "Lest we forget" must include children like Chanie Wenjack. His loss is not only a loss for our Indigenous people, but for Canada as a nation as well.

We who have not experienced such devastation cannot close our eyes to their pain. It remains as a stinking, festering sore on the history of our nation. I believe that we must act, not just as Canadians, but as humanitarians with empathy and compassion and right the wrongs of the past as best we can. And as we do, we have the opportunity to teach one another how to heal.

IT IS THE HALLMARK OF AN OPEN, ELEGANT MIND TO WELCOME AND CELEBRATE DIVERSITY...

If all you see when you look around you is your own likeness, you will never be able to recognize yourself in others. Familiarity with those who don't believe or look like we do can soften our reactions and provide insight into our own lives.

Jiddu Krishnamurti said that life is relationship. Through his wisdom you can come to understand how life is reflection, that others are a mirror in which you can see yourself—not how you *wish* others see you or how you believe others see you, but how they actually encounter you on an *energetic level*. The vibes don't lie.

As an illustration in perspective, consider how you sound to yourself when you speak and how different you sound when you hear your voice recorded. In a simplistic manner, this demonstrates that how you see yourself is one way, but not the only way.

There are many beautiful aspects of a person that are revealed only through the eyes of those who are not trained to *look* like you. Those people can be your most elegant teachers. If you truly wish to understand yourself, you must accept and appreciate all of life's teachers, not fear them.

A Constant Traveler Reminder:
HOMEWORK

• Research the true history of the Indigenous people from your country, the one that is written in their own words or told with their own voice.

• Expand your horizons. This can be as comfortable as choosing to eat at a restaurant that offers you exotic cuisine from another land, or totally breaking out of your comfort zone and taking a vacation in an exotic location that offers you a chance to learn how the locals live.

• Become familiar with your local multicultural association. Volunteer—contribute in some manner. Pay particular attention so you can learn what it is like to try to fit into a foreign culture.

• Find someone who is not at all like you, and become their friend.

45

An Elegant Mind Maintains an Attitude of Appreciation Within as Well as Without.

*It knows that when all is well within,
one is never without.*

A MASTER...

Why do we search the past to try and find a time where we have been happiest? A person can only be happy now. *Is now the happiest time of your life?*

I think about what I refer to as "tattoo moments," those moments in life that become tattooed on our memory and serve as a permanent reminder of where we've been. Our tattoo moments also allow us to appreciate how far we've come.

This is an empowering way of considering a memory. It allows us to appreciate and celebrate the great memories, as well as the not-so-great ones...*because we have survived and learned from them.*

Tattoo moments can only be appreciated and celebrated now. Celebration and appreciation naturally lead to happiness.

If a person's happiest moments were sometime in the past… that is tragic. And the tragedy continues every time we declare that our happiest moments are behind us. That can only create an unhappy future, for however long we happen to live.

There is always something colored beautiful to appreciate now.

There is life to appreciate—the opportunity to learn and grow wiser as we grow older. No matter what our age, we aren't growing younger.

There is family to love—our genetic family, as well as our soul family. Those who are living, as well as those who have died. We honor our deceased loved ones because we are better in some way for having known them. *Better can also mean wiser.*

We can appreciate waking up on this side of the grass. We can appreciate our life now and the folks in it.

Taking the time to master the elegant Art of Appreciation naturally leads to inner peace, where *all is well*.

JOE

What shall I call you?
If it matters just to me, then I shall call you Joe.
I give what I receive, and when I look around,
I see what I believe.
In every moment, Joe, you save my life.
Should I whisper this to you?
Or shout from the rooftops of your generosity?
You realize my pain, and I am whole.
Shall I give up my life to show you?
When I look into your eyes, I remember
that all is sacred space, or nothing is sacred space.
Either way, no ritual, no rite nor rote, no incense
lit as a burnt offering,

matters but just to me.
I either am, or I am not. Either way, I am what I am.
No capitalization, no reverence, no extension nor retraction,
no prostrated forms writhing in disenchanted
prayer changes that.
Words, spoken or mis-spoken are, at best, mere
symbols in a dream
and do not serve to convey what you mean to
me in your entirety.
My breath is taken by your wind, richly endowed in
its softly fired movement.
You breathe me in as I breathe out.
Here I am, Joe, content within.
At peace with these dreams.

—PDT

Things to Forget

You cannot change your destiny.

The difference between surviving and thriving is choice. Choice is power.

If you follow the rules, you will be happy.

Proving what others say is right is the fast track to misery.

If you break the rules, you will not be like others.

Rebels create a tribe of rebels. We all belong to a tribe. *Even winners and loners.*

There are winners and losers.

Winners and losers is the law of the jungle. Do you agree to adopt the vibe of this tribe?

What you think is random and has no power over what happens.

Thoughts are like boomerangs. Thoughts become words that become actions that become your life.

You have no choice when someone pushes your buttons.

There is a gap between stimulus and response. Exercise your right to live in the gap.

Only the angry survive.

Anger can be the catalyst for change. It is a healthy response to our boundaries being breached. Use anger wisely. Being angry creates an angry being.

You are powerless.

Practice like an athlete. Practice power moves by making a contingency plan for when things go sideways. Research the martial art of Aikido for further insight.

You are not enough.

Exercise your brilliance. You are no less than others because others do not see it.

Others must love you for you to love you.

There is no order of operations here. It is up to you to *feed the feeder* (this means what you feed yourself energetically). Others may love you, and you may feel it, or you may not. Or it may be hit and miss. Rock your love anyway.

THINGS TO REMEMBER

There are no rule books or assembly instructions for life.

Not for individuals or parents or kids or even for those who speak with authority. We all are doing the best we can with what we know at the time. Anyone who says they have all the answers is lying.

Society's rules are designed to keep us safe and guarantee it.

There are no guarantees. People with safety in mind get hurt and die every moment of every day.

The choices you make today change not only your future but your past from this moment on.

You read something inspirational, and you say, "Wow! That is true!" And from that moment on, you decide to make it part of the way you live your life—it becomes part of your thought system. That inspirational thing changes the way you think about the world, the way you decide what to do when you are faced with life's choices. Because of this inspiration, you make a different, more informed choice than you would have before you knew about it.

Every moment *after* you learned this new thing is different because you learned it, and in a month's time, a year's time, ten years, you will be able to think back to that moment, and you will discover something really super cool: The past month or year or ten years that you *hadn't lived* when you first had that WOW! moment has now passed, and that inspiration has changed your life!

Yes, your future will be changed because of it, but so is *any past that you will live from that moment on*. You can learn and grow and change what *will pass*, what *will be* your past, and when you look back on it, you will be able to clearly see your progress.

A Constant Traveler Reminder:
CONTINUAL LEARNING

The world's most influential and successful people are insatiable learners. They have taught themselves the art of continual improvement, of stretching their limits and challenging their thoughts. They question everything, and if something makes sense, they chew on it for a while. Then, if it works, they incorporate it into their lives. They understand that it is through insight that they reach the next level of personal growth and enlightenment. They know that opportunity flows to those who are prepared to receive it.

They understand that success is when insight meets opportunity.

Become a WOW! moment junkie…

46

An Elegant Mind Sees the Extraordinary in the Ordinary.

There is beauty in the mundane aspects of life. Beauty is all around us.

This does not mean you should focus on every detail, over-analyze, and over-think everything. It means that in every moment of life, there is something colored beautiful, but we must train our eyes to see it.

Everything looks different when we take a moment and just look, when we consider its elegant lines and innate symmetry, how every molecule of its composition is exactly as it is, in perfect harmony, if we appreciate each one for simply being part of our day. We can learn to appreciate the energy and care and attention that went into the creation of each creation, the elegant nature of nature, and most especially when we appreciate the elegance of our ultimate teacher—our own life.

If we consider only the highs of life as being noteworthy, we would be living low for most of our lives....

A Constant Traveler Reminder:
ENGAGE YOUR PET GURUS

KITTY ZEN
The nature of kitty is what she is,
moment by moment.
Nothing, more or less,
to kitty.
She has no time for such pursuits.

Every critter has so much to teach us about patience, loyalty, freedom, and compassion. I consider cats and dogs to be my furry gurus, but we can also have feathered, scaly, or crawly gurus.

Kitties demand attention, and their demands can be turned into an exercise in mindfulness. I call it the *Petting the Kitty Contemplation*, but it can just as easily be adapted to any pet that you can interact with in this manner. It only takes five minutes of your time:

Drop everything. Give the kitty your undivided attention for the full five minutes.

Observe:

- The shape of his eyes
- The shape of his ears
- The shape and length of his tail
- His coloration (does he have distinctive stripes or patches?)
  - How would you describe his color (be specific)?
  - What color is his nose, the outline of his eyes?
  - What color are his claws?
  - The pads of his feet?
- Examine his markings as if he's been gone for a year and you had to pick him out of a roomful of cats with very much the same coloration, coat, and weight.
- Feel his fur. Observe how he shows you that he enjoys your touch.
- Purr-haps your cat likes you to pet him for a short while only.
  - How does his breaking off the session make you feel?
  - Does he like to be held, or do you have to wait until he comes to you?
  - What do you think about having to wait for him to come to you?
  - Can you accept these things, or on some level do you feel rejected?

This exercise, in some manner, can be done with any pet. You can even contemplate a Chia Pet or a Pet Rock, if that "floats your boat."

47

An Elegant Mind Knows That Taking the High Road Leads to the Most Beautiful Vistas.

THE NATURE OF GENTILITY

Gentle women, gentle men
of elegant design
surely and effectively describe
the wonders of this
curious place
in which they came to
life.

—PDT

THE DANCE...

A few years ago, I had a wonderful dream. I was simply dancing. I say "simply" because it seemed like that was all I was— the dance. I remember leaping into the air with the grace of a gazelle, floating on currents of air as if in flight. I remember twisting and turning with such ease, very much like a flock of birds that somehow knows when to change direction in unison, in one multitudinous breath.

I had never felt so free, so light and ethereal. Even as I enjoyed the gossamer sensation of movement, I knew that in this body I would never feel that way. But somehow it did not matter, because that was not the objective of the dream. The real delight of it was that I was simply dancing for joy.

Truly, nothing mattered. It felt spectacular. Otherworldly. Miraculous. And deeply natural. *I remember.*

It could have become just another wonderful memory, but it really felt too good to let go of that easily. It ignited a fire of desire to live there and dance again, and again, and again.... And now I know just the place to find it. I may not be a dancer, but I know where to go to feel like one. There are times I wake up and I am already here. Other times, I just sit and patiently wait.

Sometimes your actions speak so loudly you cannot even hear your own voice. You don't know it very well at all, and you think the monkey chatter you hear every waking moment of your life is it.

IT ISN'T...

This voice will not interject. It will not shout. It will not overwhelm. You must be silent and listen. I know that if you listen, it is still there.

CALL IT INSPIRATION...

You don't have to wait for it to come; it is ready and waiting to flow in and manifest in multitudinous, effervescent expression, released through your grateful heart. Simply join in the dance. You will find that you are a much better dancer when you let inspiration lead.

A Constant Traveler Reminder:
QUALITY OF LIFE

The questions on this questionnaire begin with a statement followed by two opposite answers. Numbers extend from one extreme to its opposite. Please circle the number between 0 and 10 that indicates what is true for you. There are no right or wrong answers.

Example:

I am satisfied with my pie-making skills.

Not at all 0 1 2 3 4 5 6 7 8 9 10 Totally satisfied

Never made a pie = 0
Watched someone make a pie = 1–3
Helped someone make a pie = 4–6
Make good pies = 7–9
Make exceptional pies = 10

(continued)

At this point in your life, how satisfied are you with the following:

1. **I actively pursue my dreams and aspirations.**
   Not at all 0 1 2 3 4 5 6 7 8 9 10 Totally satisfied

2. **I make enough time for my family.**
   Not at all 0 1 2 3 4 5 6 7 8 9 10 Totally satisfied

3. **I make time for my friends and to cultivate friendships.**
   Not at all 0 1 2 3 4 5 6 7 8 9 10 Totally satisfied

4. **I tell my loved ones "I love you" regularly.**
   Not at all 0 1 2 3 4 5 6 7 8 9 10 Totally satisfied

5. **I speak my mind instead of holding back and resenting things.**
   Not at all 0 1 2 3 4 5 6 7 8 9 10 Totally satisfied

6. **I address and resolve my problems.**
   Not at all 0 1 2 3 4 5 6 7 8 9 10 Totally satisfied

7. **I am happy with my choices when I think about having children.**
   Not at all 0 1 2 3 4 5 6 7 8 9 10 Totally satisfied

8. **I save money and am preparing for retirement.**
   Not at all 0 1 2 3 4 5 6 7 8 9 10 Totally satisfied

9. **I live courageously and truthfully.**
   Not at all 0 1 2 3 4 5 6 7 8 9 10 Totally satisfied

10. **I understand that happiness is a choice.**
   Not at all 0 1 2 3 4 5 6 7 8 9 10 Totally satisfied

Add all the circled numbers.

Total Score: _____ %

Consider your score in terms of percentage of life satisfaction to date. Are you satisfied with your score? Are there areas of your life that require your care and concern?

48

An Elegant Mind Accepts the Transitions of Life.

It accepts that the way of life must include letting go in order to move forward.

ELEGANT TRANSITIONS ARE ACTS OF COURAGE...

More than one person I know spent their 30th birthday in bed. They were so bummed out by waking up on this side of the grass that they could not bring themselves to inhabit the land of the living that day. If you are reading this, then you have already made some of the transitions of life. You have moved from childhood to young adulthood. Perhaps you have moved into mature adulthood. Perhaps you are now experiencing elder adulthood. You came to life, now you are alive, and one day you will die. No ifs, ands, or buts. When your turn comes around, you will have no say in the matter. This prospect can be terrifying.

The only stage in life that we actually *look forward* to is the one from childhood to young adulthood. After that, we begin to resist each day with more and more energy. In an effort to deny the progress of time, we begin looking back more and more.

Deny it, we may, but that does not change the fact that we are being delivered from one moment to the next with shocking surety. Why the shock? Each stage in life is marked by a transition into the next and represents an end of a familiar order and a beginning of a new, unknown order. The unknown scares the snot out of us.

AN INDICATOR OF YOUR POTENTIAL FOR SUCCESS IS HOW WELL YOU ACCEPT THESE TRANSITIONS...

The Transition Energy Balance of Give/Receive

STAGE OF LIFE	ENERGY FLOW	TRANSITION CHALLENGE
1. Childhood	Receive	Accept without entitlement as an elegant student

During this stage, your willingness to learn, receive love and an education from others, and gather resources and skills, affects your ability to grow and meet your future needs.

2. Young Adult	Give	Share without arrogance or conditional terms as an elegant instructor

During this stage you have opportunities to demonstrate excellence in career and work, parenting, and citizenship.

3. Mature Adult	Give	Share without resentment as an elegant contributor

During this stage you offer wisdom and experience as a mentor, grandparent, or caregiver.

STAGE OF LIFE	ENERGY FLOW	TRANSITION CHALLENGE
4. Elder Adult	Receive	Accept gracefully without regret as an elegant legacy builder

During this stage you see the reality of a life well lived as a loving grandparent, respected citizen in the community, and/or esteemed benefactor who exemplifies wisdom, dignity, and acceptance.

A Constant Traveler Reminder:
MAKE ELEGANT TRANSITIONS

Every transition period offers you a unique opportunity to re-evaluate your values, beliefs, and assumptions and to adjust your attitude toward this next stage of life.

1. Identify your next transition.
- With a spirit of acceptance, reframe the idea of using this next stage as an opportunity for growth.

2. Identify and challenge your fears, worries, and anxieties.
- What scares you about your next stage of life?
- What support and/or resources can you gather to make this transition go smoothly?

(continued)

3. Simplify.
- Minimize the complexity and confusion through clarification.
- What is important to you at this stage of life?
- What can you release, pass on, or relinquish?
- Who is important in this new stage?

4. Identify the tasks and opportunities of your new role.
- What are your objectives?
- How would you enjoy living at this stage?
- What will be the best part of this stage of your life?
- What are you willing to change?
- What will change with or without your agreement?

We come into this world with nothing,
and we will leave this world with just as much...

49

An Elegant Mind Beholds the Mirror That Reflects Both the Pleasant and Unpleasant Aspects of Life.

It recognizes what is reflected through
the eyes of compassion.

Two women are talking. They agree that the deer grazing in the field nearby are beautiful—their slender bodies lithe and streamlined; large ears that magically brighten quizzical, gentle faces; warm tan coats designed to blend so beautifully with the trees and quiet forest glens; dark, expressive, reflecting-pool eyes, so lovely and so tragic when they are reduced to just another object in front of a car...or caught in the crosshairs of a hunter's life-and-death decision.

"But moose," one woman scoffs. "Moose are ugly." Her face goes hard as she thinks of their huge, shaggy-square bodies and long, dark faces hiding seldom-seen eyes, wild as maniacs and unpredictable as death as they smash into cars and chase unwary hikers. She didn't care what happened to ugly moose.

The other woman thought of the soft, warm muzzle of a cow moose as it licks its newborn calf, her life-giving, velvet-teated udder as the calf struggles to its feet and suckles.

"Moose are beautiful to moose," she gently replied.

Fast-forward a thousand years, it seems. The gentlewoman is standing at a crossroads that reflects the crosshairs of another hunter's gun. She watches as beauty enters the room. It arrives on four legs, wrapped in dark brown fur. It wiggles its hind end with pleasure, docked tail cut tight. It wears a collar with an inscription that reads "*Étoile*," meaning "star" in English.

Étoile is indeed a star. She carries herself with a demure elegance that the woman recognizes as her nature. It is inexhaustible.

There is an empty chair between two men of the women's group. The dog gently and gracefully climbs up, turns around, and sits on the chair beside them. She turns to the first man and bids him welcome in her language, with doe eyes soft and gentle, offering a nuzzle and a pleasant lick for his face. He cannot stand to look at her let alone touch her. He leans away, grimacing.

Nonplussed, Étoile turns to the man on her opposite side. She is unruffled by the first man's reaction. She understands that it is always time to begin again.

"What an ugly dog!" the second man says with a laugh. "Dogs like you are too ugly to live." His smile is a caricature of kindness as he scratches her ears.

She knows a few words—"good," "car," "pee," "walk," "toy"—but she is what she is. She is the best dog she knows.

Perhaps she cannot understand why he is laughing. Or perhaps, somewhere in her open animal heart, she can understand that if he had his way, she would not be alive. Not her kind. Either way, she forgives him for it. And ugly words transform in one swipe of a canine master's tongue.

The woman smiles into this grace-filled moment. She is overcome by gratitude for having the eyes to see the beauty of its teacher.

The mirror is clear: Beauty and ugliness reflect the light in the exact. Same. Manner. It reveals in elegant detail stars where man sees ugliness, as well as the ugliness in what man has come to behold as stars.

WHAT YOU SEE DEPENDS ON
HOW YOU BOW YOUR HEAD...

A Constant Traveler Reminder:
SOMETHING COLORED BEAUTIFUL

Challenge yourself to identify something (or someone) colored beautiful in each hour of this day. Look for someone or something that you would normally find distasteful or look away from. Persist until you identify its beauty.

Set your watch, the timer on your computer, or an alarm on your phone to go off at regular intervals as a reminder.

50

An Elegant Mind Knows That Silence Hears Its Own Voice.

Being Silent

If you cannot be silent, you cannot listen.
If you cannot listen, you cannot be a true parent,
or lover, or friend.

If you cannot be silent, you cannot be calm.
If you cannot be calm, you are at the whim of distraction.

If you cannot be silent, you cannot grow.
If you cannot grow, you cannot grow wise.

If you cannot be silent, you cannot learn.
If you cannot learn, you cannot achieve mastery.

If you cannot be silent, you cannot hear
the voice of inspiration.
If you cannot hear the voice of inspiration,
you cannot dream.

If you cannot be silent, you cannot be silenced.
If you cannot be silenced, you will always be afraid.

If you cannot be silent, you cannot find peace.
And regretfully, peace can never find you.

—PDT

A Constant Traveler Reminder:
THE SOUND OF SILENCE EXERCISE

What if we thought of silence as breath, like the effort-less breathing of life in and life out? When we truly listen for our breath, we naturally fall silent. Perhaps this is the subtlest aspect of voice?

1. Sit comfortably. Place one hand on your heart. Feel your hand as it rests on the space right over your heart.

2. Gently place your other hand on your abdomen (just below your rib cage). Feel the support of both hands. You are safe.

3. Relax your hands and arms. Close your eyes, if you wish (this may help you focus).

4. Inhale slowly through your nose, focusing on moving the hand that is on your abdomen.

5. Inhale until you cannot comfortably take in more air.

6. Hold your breath for one second.

7. Exhale softly through your mouth or nose. As you exhale, tighten your stomach muscles.

8. Exhale until you cannot comfortably continue to breathe out. Don't force the breath.

9. Hold for one second.

Continue breathing this way for five minutes. Work your way up to 10 minutes. There are no rules. Keep your eyes closed, or use a candle as your focus. Listen for the flow of your breath.

Learn to be silent. And you'll notice you talk too much.
—Ajahn Brahm, Buddhist monk

51

An Elegant Mind Knows That Its Best Life Teaching Is by Living Its Best Life.

What if I told you that the last third of your life can be your absolute best? Would you believe me? What if I told you that you can feel more fulfilled, find more meaning, and establish more connections than ever before? Would you believe me? If I said that you can feel good, look good, and contribute more to your community in a way that leaves each day better than the one before, would you believe me? Would you believe me if I said it depends on what you believe?

If you are familiar with the story of *Alice in Wonderland*, then perhaps the idea of following this White Rabbit is about as appealing as admitting that you are eligible for the Senior's Day discount at Walmart.

LIVING YOUR BEST LIFE AT ANY AGE
MEANS NOT PRETENDING.

It is not a fantasy that lands you at the Mad Hatter's Tea Party, pretending to be a young person. The truth is, if you are not already there, the day will come when you wake up "older." Older than younger. Whatever stage of life you are experiencing, this moment may be your last chance (and possibly first opportunity) to be exactly who you are.

One day it dawned on me that I was afraid of tomorrow. What if tomorrow never comes? Who would I be then? Or what if it does come and it is painful? I realized that I was grasping at life with one hand and pushing it away with the other—a totally confusing and disorienting exercise. I realized that I was perennially living in fear. Every thought I had was weighed against the risks involved, measured by the rules, boundaries, and limitations I had set up to circumnavigate the fears and challenges of my life.

This wasn't fantasy. I wasn't pretending to be scared—I was scared. And I realized I wasn't alone.

WHY DO WE WORK AT LIVING LONG
BUT HATE LIVING LONG?

We Baby Boomers have enormous power in the marketplace. The balance has tipped to where the people born in the period immediately after World War II (and up until approximately 1965) are now driving the bus in our consumer-driven society. Over the past decade, the media has been gradually getting on board, focusing on marketing to aging bodies, aging minds, and Boomer lifestyles.

However, our old-boy's clubbing, youth-oriented, anti-aging culture has also produced casualties. Consider a product designed to enhance aging skin being represented by a model who is young enough to be the target market's daughter or granddaughter. Consider a 20- or 30-something flashing her lack of years into the camera, reassuring the 40-, 50-, 60-, and 70-somethings that "we will get 100% gray coverage."

More recently, public resistance to these advertisements (that incite women older than 30 to purchase their product at the expense of not only their pocketbook but also their self-worth) has forced companies to use older models—*models they choose very selectively for their youthful appearance.*

It is reasonable for a company to choose a person who meets the current standard of physical appeal to represent its brand. However, we, as aging consumers, must realize that it is up to us to dictate what we will accept. We do it by our purchases. It seems we like what these models are selling.

Baby Boomers are a force of nature. The evidence is clear. A multibillion-dollar anti-aging industry holds the burden of proof.

We are as "anti-aging" as is the youth we value. We pretend to accept it, while we mount a subtle resistance movement beginning in as early as our 20s, proving that the more years we spend on this side of the grass, the less we value that time.

WE HAVE LEARNED TO LIVE UPSIDE-DOWN AND OUTSIDE-IN...

Consider that we are always representing something to someone. Are we demonstrating our personal brand of apology for getting older? We tell our kids to dream big while we tell them stories of how we once dreamed but didn't make it. Are we demonstrating that dreams no longer apply to us? Or are we living our dream—our dream of what the world looks like for our kid's parent? Or grandparent?

Ashton Applewhite says that ageism is the last acceptable prejudice. What if we simply lived each day as it comes along, without comparisons to the days of youth that we enjoyed yesterday? Without the comparisons we make to those younger, faster, healthier, smarter, more attractive, or more talented? Our youthful tendency to compare ourselves to our peers has morphed into our personal version of ageism.

What have we learned from our time on this rock? I think it's time to rock our wise!

WHEN I LABEL ME, I CREATE ME...

Who do you think taught you to look at aging this way?

Who do you think teaches the younger generations how to treat their elders?

Who do you think has the power to change how you think and what you think?

CHANGE THE WAY YOU THINK ABOUT AGING, AND CHANGE THE WAY YOU AGE.

What is the age of well-being? You are either old or future-old. There is a difference between becoming an elder (mentor, guide, wise one) and becoming elderly. You can choose to be a dignified, vibrant, engaged, and elegant elder. You can be an example for those who follow you into old age.

A Constant Traveler Reminder:
ACT YOUR AGE

Do you believe that what you see demonstrated in your life by others has a potent influence on you? Test your hypothesis:

What is your vision of old age?
- Is it the vision your parents and grandparents are living now?
- Do you wish to live like they do?
- If they are living a vibrant, joyful life, what a wonderful gift they have given you!
- If not, how could you craft an alternative vision for your future?

How do you talk about old age? Examine your current vernacular regarding aging:
- Elder vs. elderly
- Older vs. old
- Honor vs. sympathy
- Respect vs. contempt

How do you talk about elders when they are not within earshot?

52

An Elegant Mind Knows That True Humility Means Being Honest About Its Weakness.

Humility is living in a manner that demonstrates that you cannot know it all and by accepting the idea that the thing you don't know, as Neale Donald Walsch says, may be the idea that changes everything.

Humility is understanding that we can grasp the concept of the whole picture, but we cannot truly understand the whole picture. We see in snapshots.

Life is relationship. We need one another because others show us to ourselves. The story about a lone wolf thriving without the pack is a myth.

Humility is the ability to appreciate and perceive value in others as well as in ourselves. Humility does not discount its strengths. It does not dictate that you devalue your innate talents but use them for the benefit of one and all.

What is is your talent. Denying this is ego, not humility.

ACCEPT VALUE FOR VALUE. THERE IS NOTHING HUMBLE
ABOUT DENYING YOUR NATURAL TALENTS AND SKILLS
BY NOT ACCEPTING THEIR BENEFITS...

Creative reframing (revising our life story) requires humility.
We must be able to admit that we may have gotten it wrong.
Humility is acquiescence to what is, and acting in line with it.

Humility is also admitting:

• That you are not above the natural laws that govern all life
and that you cannot circumvent them.

• That you cannot break life's natural laws without consequences. Even "The Great" are subject to gravity.

• That you are required to develop a vibrant inner life so you
are governed and regulated by a conscience aligned with what is.

• When you are out of alignment with what is. You must be
open to inspiration and be willing to investigate all mirrors that
show you to yourself.

• That the anger, resentment, and regret generated by the
shoulda, coulda, wouldas do not serve you.

• That you are responsible and take authentic accountability
for your actions.

• That it is better to be a learn-it-all than a know-it-all. Even
the greatest among us cannot know it all.

Be honest about your weaknesses, and then find other people who complement them—those who are strong in the areas in which you are not. Then, as a team, play to your collective strengths.

As a team player, you humbly admit that by yourself you can accomplish nothing of lasting value. Even the most successful of us have a team supporting them. You cannot know or be it all.

Interdependence is relationship's highest form. It is a mutually beneficial, complementary, balancing equilibrium that promotes the exchange of energies. Any successful alliance is a win-win.

AN INTERDEPENDENT RELATIONSHIP CANNOT HAPPEN IF EACH PARTNER USES THEIR STRENGTHS IN DEFENSE OF THEIR PERSONAL WEAKNESSES.

You protect your weaknesses at the expense of your strengths, wasting precious energy and resources in their defense as you struggle to compete with the other's natural strengths.

A successful relationship is one in which each person knows their personal strengths, values the other's personal strengths, and offers them the freedom to do what they do best by elegantly moving out of their way. They support each other's weaknesses and play to their innate strengths. They celebrate each other in these endeavors. The other person always strives to do their best in all respects, but understand that *when you know what you do best, you live best.*

You don't have to reinvent the wheel. All you need to do is relax and roll with it.

A Constant Traveler Reminder:
INSPIRATION, CONNECTION, AND CONTRIBUTION EXERCISE

• **Where can you find the means to create a mind-spark of inspiration this week?**

Suggestion: Reading is a fantastic means of creating mind-sparks! So are TED Talks! https://www.ted.com/

• **How can you strengthen one relationship this week?**

Suggestion: Make a date with your significant other, or organize a night out with a friend.

• **How can you contribute to the collective strength of your community this week?**

Suggestion: Attend a municipal community event, volunteer to work at a festival, or attend an event sponsored by your local multicultural association.

Your Elegant Mind...

Whatever the mind is taught to expect, that it will build,
produce, and bring forth for you.
—Catherine Ponder

It is easy to read the wisdom books and memorize the correct terms. I have learned from experience that it is much easier to talk the talk than it is to walk the walk. Many times, when we say we know something, it means that we understand it intellectually, but knowing something intellectually and *actually living* this way are two different things.

What if, for example, you substituted the word *know* as in *I know how to live with an elegant mind*, with the word *live* as in *I live with an elegant mind every day*...would the statement still be true for you?

What if, in the words of Aerosmith, you were to *Walk This Way*?

People who live with an elegant mind know its true value. They practice it so they can feel it. They share it so they can continue feeling it.

Up until this point, your consciousness has been fed with ingredients that can evolve into an elegant mind. It's up to you to take the next steps—to begin a dialogue and make friends with your Constant Traveler. To discover your personal elegance.

Whether you randomly choose one or two of these lessons, return to a specific lesson that touched something deep inside of you, or work on all of them, in turn...consider each to be a wonderful experience in and of itself.

Regardless of your age, approach each with the curiosity of a child, with a beginner's mind, as this may be the beginning of your next beautiful friendship or lifelong love.

That reminds me…I invite you to return to the very first lesson, on page 9. It's a big one that you'll always want to remember.

I thank you, in advance, for sharing.

—PDT

Quotes

Page 5: "Between stimulus and response there is a space. In that space is our power to choose our response. In our response lies our growth and our freedom." —Viktor E. Frankl

Page 11: "Eventually, you will come to understand that love heals everything, and love is all there is." —Gary Zukav

Page 25: "As you breathe in, cherish yourself. As you breathe out, cherish all Beings." —His Holiness the Dalai Lama

Page 29: "God sleeps in the minerals, awakens in plants, walks in animals, and thinks in man." —Arthur Young

Page 35: "We need to remember that circumstances don't make a person, they reveal a person." —Emma Jameson

Page 41: "Perfectionism is just a delay logic fancied up to look respectable." —Brendon Burchard

Page 54: "When was the last time you did something for the first time?" —John C. Maxwell

Page 62: "If the only prayer you ever say in your entire life is thank you, it will be enough." —Meister Eckhart

Page 63: "Life is so very difficult. How can we be anything but kind?" Jack Kornfield

Page 65: "If it's natural to kill, how come men have to go into training to learn how?" —Joan Baez

Page 71: "There is no path to peace. Peace is the path." —Gandhi

Page 75: "Low-key change helps the human mind circum-navigate the fear that blocks success and creativity."
—Robert Maurer

Page 92: "When you label me, you negate me."
—Soren Kierkegaard

Page 101: "Anxiety is the handmaiden of contemporary ambition." —Alain de Botton

Page 104: "Failure is learned behavior." —Bishop TD Jakes

Page 108: "Today's Declaration: My word is LAW." —T. Harv Eker

Page 109: "May you taste your words before you spit them out." —Irish proverb

Page 131: "Invictus" —William Ernest Henley, 1888

Page 145: "May you never forget what is worth remembering nor ever remember what is best forgotten." —Irish blessing

Page 173: "Name the greatest of all inventors. Accident." —Mark Twain

Page 175: "Be happy with what you have, and you will have plenty to be happy about." —Irish proverb

Page 181: "If you lose the power to laugh, you lose the power to think." —Clarence Darrow

Page 182: "A good laugh and a long sleep are the two best cures for anything." —Irish proverb

Page 215: "If we were supposed to speak more than we hear, then we'd have two mouths and only one ear" —Mark Twain

Page 251: "Learn to be silent. And you'll notice you talk too much." —Ajahn Brahm, Buddhist monk

Page 265: "Whatever the mind is taught to expect, that it will build, produce, and bring forth for you." —Catherine Ponder

Resources

Covey, Stephen R. *The 7 Habits of Highly Effective People: Powerful Lessons in Personal Change.* New York: Simon & Schuster, 1989.

Ruiz, Miguel. *The Four Agreements: A Practical Guide to Personal Freedom.* San Rafael, CA: Amber-Allen Publishing, 1997.

Ware, Bronnie. *The Top Five Regrets of the Dying—A Life Transformed by the Dearly Departing.* Carlsbad: Hay House Inc., reprint edition, March 20, 2012.